WORKING WITH NUMBERS

09-BTO-449

AUTHOR
James T. Shea

CONSULTANT
Susan L. Beutel
Consulting/Resource Teacher
Lamoille North Supervisory Union, VT

ACKNOWLEDGEMENTS

Senior Math Editor: Karen L. Lassiter

Project Coordinator: Cynthia Ellis

Project Design and Development:
The Wheetley Company

Cover Design: Robin Bouvette
Cover Illustration: Danal Terry

WORKING WITH NUMBERS SERIES:

Level A/Point	Level D/Rectangle	Consumer
Level B/Line	Level E/Pentagon	Refresher
Level C/Triangle	Level F/Hexagon	Algebra

ISBN: 0-8114-4239-X

Steck-Vaughn Company
A Subsidiary of National Education Corporation

1 2 3 4 5 6 7 8 9 0 HG 95 94 93 92 91 90

TABLE OF CONTENTS

Unit 5 • Driving a Car

Unit 6 • Owning a Home

Unit 7 • Paying Taxes

REVIEWING BASIC SKILLS

Reading and Writing Numbers

A place-value chart can help you read and write whole numbers and decimals. Each digit in a number has a value based on its place in the number.

We read and write the number in the place-value chart as: four hundred fifty-two thousand, five hundred twenty-one and six hundred thirteen thousandths.

Notice that commas are used to separate the digits into groups of three. This helps make larger numbers easier to read.

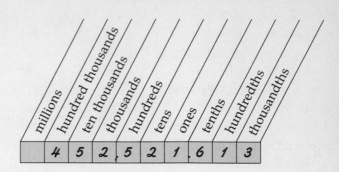

millions	hundred thousands	ten thousands	thousands	hundreds	tens	ones	tenths	hundredths	thousandths
4	5	2	5	2	1	6	1	3	

Write each number in the place-value chart.

1. 7,646,918.764

2. 189,498.004

3. 96,950.53

4. $2000.99

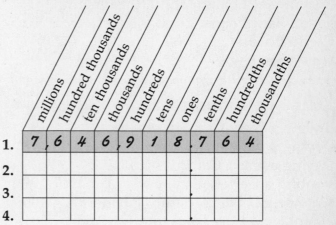

	millions	hundred thousands	ten thousands	thousands	hundreds	tens	ones	tenths	hundredths	thousandths
1.	7	6	4	6	9	1	8	7	6	4
2.										
3.										
4.										

Write each number using digits. Insert commas where needed.

5. ninety-nine and one hundredth _____ *99.01* _____

6. fifty-six thousand, forty-seven and thirty-one hundredths _____

7. forty-two dollars and fifty-three cents _____

8. eight and six hundred twelve thousandths _____

Write each number in words. Insert commas where needed.

9. 50.8 _____ *fifty and eight tenths* _____

10. 816.07 _____

11. 385.41 _____

_____

12. 1005.075 _____

_____

13. $13.99 _____

14. $210.35 _____

Comparing and Ordering

To compare two numbers, begin at the left.
Compare the digits in each place.

Remember,
- zeros at the end of a decimal do not change the value of the decimal.

$$2 = 2.0 = 2.00$$
$$2.2 = 2.20$$

- you can write zeros so that the numbers have the same number of places.

Compare. Write <, >, or =.

	a	b	c
1.	58 __>__ 52	48 _____ 48.0	88 _____ 62
	5 8 / 5 2	4 8 / 4 8 . 0	8 8 / 6 2
2.	183 _____ 95	21 _____ 215	37 _____ 37.0
	1 8 3 / 9 5	2 1 / 2 1 5	3 7 / 3 7 . 0
3.	0.789 _____ 0.7	2399.9 _____ 2400.0	9.8 _____ 9.20
4.	23.56 _____ 28	689 _____ 689.1	345.987 _____ 895.67

Write in order from least to greatest.

5. 76   45   98 ___ *45   76   98* ___

6. 789   287   891 _____

7. 190   754   561 _____

8. 3963   9867   1256 _____

9. 8432   2876   8765 _____

10. 78.67   84.13   32.85 ___ *32.85   78.67   84.13* ___

11. 375.2   973.9   24.678 _____

12. 0.674   0.340   0.970 _____

13. 12.976   12.975   12.97 _____

14. 7.6   4.5   9.8 _____

15. 190   1.90   0.190 _____

5

Rounding

Often you will need to round numbers to estimate or to make a problem easier to understand.

Remember, 5 or greater rounds up.

Round to the nearest ten.

	a	b	c	d
1.	45 _50_	87 _____	93 _____	21 _____
2.	478 _____	311 _____	3255 _____	4189 _____

Round to the nearest hundred.

	a	b	c	d
3.	521 _500_	670 _____	427 _____	752 _____
4.	4350 _____	5375 _____	11,755 _____	68,906 _____

Round to the nearest tenth.

	a	b	c	d
5.	9.34 _9.3_	7.27 _____	3.55 _____	45.67 _____
6.	1.111 _____	4.932 _____	22.760 _____	39.129 _____

Round to the nearest hundredth.

	a	b	c	d
7.	2.831 _2.83_	15.947 _____	6.295 _____	81.608 _____
8.	4.9023 _____	0.6105 _____	1.8264 _____	0.0995 _____

Round to the nearest dollar.

	a	b	c	d
9.	$24.25 _$24_	$24.75 _____	$39.99 _____	$95.95 _____
10.	$329.87 _____	$836.49 _____	$1120.95 _____	$1999.95 _____

Addition and Subtraction of Whole Numbers

Add. Regroup when necessary.

	a	b	c	d	e
1.	4 7 4 + 2 3 2 **7 0 6**	3 0 5 + 7 6	1 4 8 + 5 1 6	2 6 + 7 8 1	9 5 0 + 3 9 4
2.	8 9 2 + 8 9 0 2	6 5,9 8 7 + 3 9,7 6 0	1 2,8 9 6 + 9 0,6 4 2	6 5 4 0 + 3 6 1	4 3,1 7 9 + 5,0 8 7
3.	7 8 9 3 8 0 9 3 + 1 5 6 3	9 8,4 5 3 4,7 2 1 + 7 5,2 3 0	7,5 4 3 5 9,9 3 2 + 6,0 8 1	8 3 9 1 2,4 7 6 + 5,3 9 0	7 2,1 6 6 2 0 5 + 3 1,6 5 4

Subtract. Regroup when necessary.

	a	b	c	d	e
4.	7 6 4 − 1 5 6 **6 0 8**	5 6 2 − 4 8	8 2 9 1 − 7 8 3	1 9 3 6 4 7 9	4 3 0 1 − 2 9 9 9
5.	4 5,0 0 0 3 4,0 2 9	5 4,7 6 4 6,9 8 7	9 0,7 6 0 − 3 9,2 6 3	1 1 9,0 7 6 − 1 1 8,9 9 9	1 3,8 2 1 − 4,2 9 6
6.	7 2,5 4 1 − 5,3 1 6	8 4,2 0 5 − 3 7,0 0 9	9 2,6 4 0 − 8,7 2 1	5 0,0 1 3 − 6,8 3 5	1 0,0 0 0 − 4,9 9 9

Line up the digits. Then add or subtract. Regroup when necessary.

	a	b	c
7.	$6573 + 34 =$ _____	$746 - 347 =$ _____	$46,527 + 547,907 =$ _____

6573
+ 34

Addition and Subtraction of Decimals

Add. Write zeros as needed.

	a	*b*	*c*	*d*	*e*
1.	7.20 +5.47 *12.67*	60.9 +37.6	15.4 +93.2	8 +1.7	6.7 +1.9
2.	$3.48 + 0.49	$892.10 + 1.73	$12.92 + 67.02	$10.66 + 19.29	$1.99 + 0.57
3.	75.93 401.3 +1561	7845.3 4462.1 +8752.27	397.543 269.31 +3135.8	17.431 90.459 + 8.02	63.95 0.08 +9

Subtract. Write zeros as needed.

	a	*b*	*c*	*d*	*e*
4.	$\overset{7\ \ 10}{8}.\cancel{0}$ −6.6 *1.4*	7.24 −3.47	8.9 −4	6.15 −0.09	12 − 5.1
5.	$892.10 − 0.78	$2600.75 − 340.29	$557.63 − 6.98	$190.76 − 14.99	$300 − 37.58
6.	9056.3 − 32.76	3.729 −0.086	8.4 −2.173	62.143 − 9.5	4.01 −2.107

Line up the digits. Write zeros as needed. Then add or subtract.

	a	*b*	*c*
7.	65.73 − 0.34 = _____	734 − 44.7 = _____	709.8 + 807.87 = _____

65.73
− 0.34

Estimation of Sums and Differences

Estimate the sum or difference to the nearest ten.

	a	b	c	d
1.	$139\rightarrow$ *140* $+\ 53\rightarrow +\ 50$ *190*	$821\rightarrow$ $+9853\rightarrow$	$6789\rightarrow$ $-2345\rightarrow$	$129{,}201\rightarrow$ $-\ 45{,}679\rightarrow$

Estimate the sum or difference to the nearest hundred.

	a	b	c	d
2.	$7878\rightarrow$ *7900* $+\ 621\rightarrow +\ 600$ *8500*	$13{,}542\rightarrow$ $+67{,}890\rightarrow$	$8943\rightarrow$ $-6785\rightarrow$	$12{,}641\rightarrow$ $-\ 9{,}870\rightarrow$

Estimate the sum or difference to the nearest one.

	a	b	c	d
3.	$\$\ \ \ 1.99\rightarrow\$\ \ \ 2$ $12.19\rightarrow\ \ \ 12$ $+\ 110.79\rightarrow +111$ $\$125$	$\$\ 31.47\rightarrow$ $568.76\rightarrow$ $+\ \ \ 23.98\rightarrow$	$\$57.48\rightarrow$ $-\ 32.40\rightarrow$	$\$82.72\rightarrow$ $-\ 64.02\rightarrow$

Estimate the sum or difference to the nearest tenth.

	a	b	c	d
4.	$20.01\rightarrow$ *20.0* $+69.29\rightarrow +69.3$ *89.3*	$50.75\rightarrow$ $+73.94\rightarrow$	$8.56\rightarrow$ $-6.25\rightarrow$	$3.44\rightarrow$ $-0.89\rightarrow$

Estimate the sum or difference to the nearest hundredth.

	a	b	c	d
5.	$2.379\rightarrow$ *2.38* $+0.026\rightarrow +0.03$ *2.41*	$5.342\rightarrow$ $+3.876\rightarrow$	$478.287\rightarrow$ $-235.61\ \rightarrow$	$50.621\rightarrow$ $-\ 7.878\rightarrow$

REVIEWING BASIC SKILLS

Multiplication of Whole Numbers

Multiply.

	a	b	c	d	e
	1				
1.	36	21	401	6812	89,920
	× 2	× 4	× 8	× 7	× 9
	72				

2.	52	42	59	547	4000
	×10	×58	×36	× 84	× 70

3.	186	200	539	417	263
	× 78	× 46	× 68	× 30	× 99

4.	985	544	196	702	357
	×340	×807	×532	×100	×498

Line up the digits. Then multiply.

a	b	c

5. $6573 \times 9 =$ _____ $108 \times 247 =$ _____ $56 \times 92 =$ _____

$$
\begin{array}{r}
6573 \\
\times \quad 9 \\
\hline
\end{array}
$$

6. $500 \times 41 =$ _____ $75 \times 38 =$ _____ $20 \times 96 =$ _____

Multiplication of Decimals

Multiply.

	a	b	c	d	e
1.	$\overset{2}{3}4.1$ $\times\ 2.5$ $\overline{1705}$ $682\ 0$ $\overline{85.25}$	6.7 $\times 0.8$	19.3 $\times\ 4.6$	892.5 $\times\ 73.1$	75.8 $\times 30.9$
2.	1.875 $\times\ \ \ \ \ 2$	$\$3.49$ $\times\ \ \ \ 16$	$\$68.02$ $\times\ \ \ \ \ 53$	$54,000$ $\times\ \ 0.18$	259 $\times 0.07$
3.	0.435 $\times 0.276$	0.126 $\times 0.007$	0.009 $\times 0.362$	3.078 $\times 0.901$	0.301 $\times 1.564$

Line up the digits. Then multiply.

a	b	c
4. $12.73 \times 0.54 = $ _____	$4.45 \times 3.9 = $ _____	$64,527 \times 0.09 = $ _____

12.73
$\times\ \ 0.54$

5. $5.98 \times 0.87 = $ _____	$81.7 \times 6.52 = $ _____	$29,173 \times 0.4 = $ _____

PROBLEM-SOLVING STRATEGY

Choose an Operation

Sometimes a problem does not tell you whether to add, subtract, multiply, or divide. To solve such a problem, you must read the problem carefully. Then, decide what the problem is asking you to do. Next, choose an operation to solve the problem. Finally, solve the problem.

EXAMPLE 1
Read the problem.

> Robin bought 2.35 pounds of grapes and 1.59 pounds of plums. How many pounds of fruit did she buy?

Decide what the problem is asking.

> In this problem, the question "How many pounds of fruit..." is asking you to find a total or sum.

Choose the operation.

> To solve, you must add.

Solve the problem.

> 2.35 + 1.59 = 3.94
>
> Robin bought a total of 3.94 pounds of fruit.

EXAMPLE 2
Read the problem.

> A plumber charged $608 for 19 hours of work. The charge was the same for each hour. What was the plumber's hourly rate?

Decide what the problem is asking.

> In this problem, the question "What was the ...rate?" is asking you to find equal parts.

Choose the operation.

> To solve, you must divide.

Solve the problem.

> $608 ÷ 19 = $32   The plumber's rate was $32 per hour.

Choose the operation needed to solve each problem. Then solve.

1. In April, the Randolf family spent $483 for food. This was $37 more than the amount spent in March. How much did the Randolf family spend for food in March?

   Operation _____

   Answer _____

2. In one day, 934 concert tickets were sold for $23 each. How much money was taken in from the sale of the tickets?

   Operation _____

   Answer _____

Choose the operation needed to solve each problem. Then solve.

3. How far can a bus travel in 4.5 hours if its average speed is 52 miles per hour?

Operation _____

Answer _____

4. A shoe store sold 1620 pairs of shoes in a 30-day period. What was the average number of pairs sold per day?

Operation _____

Answer _____

5. To buy a computer, Yvonne is making 36 equal payments of $54 each. What is the total of the payments?

Operation _____

Answer _____

6. Brenda drove 1329 miles in January and 1893 miles in February. How many more miles did she drive in February?

Operation _____

Answer _____

7. The payroll of one department in a certain company is $2933. Each of the 7 employees receives the same pay. What is the pay for each employee?

Operation _____

Answer _____

8. On Monday, Hal's club collected 92.3 pounds of newspapers for recycling. On Tuesday, the amount collected was 24.2 pounds more than on Monday. How much was collected on Tuesday?

Operation _____

Answer _____

9. Vernon's phone bill was $54.77 in March. In April, the bill was $6.89 less than in March. How much was the phone bill in April?

Operation _____

Answer _____

10. A card table costs $24.96 and the chairs are $11.84 each. Find the cost of the table and two chairs.

Operation _____

Answer _____

11. Ernie earned $60.32 for working 8 hours. What was the hourly rate?

Operation _____

Answer _____

12. Jessica weighs 45.7 kilograms. She weighs 4.2 kilograms more than Jenny. How much does Jenny weigh?

Operation _____

Answer _____

Division of Whole Numbers

Divide and check.

	a	b	c	d
1.	12 R27 45)567 45 117 90 27	23)543	39)303	12)6489
2.	56)785	27)678	76)564	34)8867
3.	64)7865	55)3030	40)8765	60)4320
4.	21)8442	43)4343	62)3723	39)7862

Set up the problem. Then divide and check.

	a	b	c
5.	$897 \div 2 =$ _____ 2)897	$389 \div 14 =$ _____	$2375 \div 32 =$ _____
6.	$5678 \div 54 =$ _____	$6352 \div 76 =$ _____	$1698 \div 12 =$ _____

Division of Decimals

Divide. Round to the nearest tenth if needed. Write zeros as needed.

	a	*b*	*c*	*d*

1.

$$6.8 \overline{)5.44} \quad \begin{array}{r} 0.8 \\ \end{array}$$
$$\begin{array}{r} 5\ 44 \\ \hline 0 \end{array}$$

$3 \overline{)21.3}$ $8.7 \overline{)8.874}$ $12 \overline{)64.44}$

2. $4.1 \overline{)23.616}$ $12.9 \overline{)387}$ $4.6 \overline{)12.926}$ $9.1 \overline{)88.27}$

3. $0.94 \overline{)78.02}$ $0.28 \overline{)0.364}$ $0.003 \overline{)17.736}$ $0.16 \overline{)34.88}$

4. $78 \overline{)7.8}$ $2.7 \overline{)0.216}$ $0.65 \overline{)12.61}$ $2.6 \overline{)0.3354}$

Set up the problem. Divide. Round to the nearest tenth if needed.
Write zeros as needed.

	a	*b*	*c*

5. $0.754 \div 5.8 =$ _____ $248.2 \div 34 =$ _____ $84.15 \div 0.45 =$ _____

$5.8 \overline{)0.754}$

6. $80.46 \div 2.7 =$ _____ $0.99 \div 9.9 =$ _____ $306.6 \div 1.4 =$ _____

REVIEWING BASIC SKILLS

Estimation of Products and Quotients

Estimate by rounding both numbers.

	a	b	c	d
1.	854→ *850* × 47→ × *50* *42,500*	361→ × 55→	12→ ×43→	920→ × 89→

	a	b	c	d
2.	0.85→ ×5.90→	2.1→ × 64→	0.36→ ×19.8→	93.6→ ×0.83→

Estimate using basic facts.

	a	b	c	d
3.	*120* 4)465→ 4)480	3)341→	7)746→	2)453→

	a	b	c	d
4.	8)4.97→	4)390→	6)25.4→	5)1.76→

Estimate by rounding both numbers.

	a	b	c	d
5.	*15* 54)746→ 50)750	78)315→	15)602→	83)721→

	a	b	c	d
6.	8.5)355→	0.53)2.97→	89)362→	5.8)3.64→

REVIEWING BASIC SKILLS
Calculator Applications

A calculator can help you understand place value. Any standard number can be written as hundreds, tens, tenths, hundredths, and so on.

EXAMPLE 1 230 = _____ hundreds

Divide 230 by 100 mentally. Think of moving the decimal point.

230 = ___2.3___ hundreds

Check the answer with a calculator.

230 ÷ 100 = | 2.3 |

EXAMPLE 2 5.281 = _____ tenths

Dividing by 0.1 is the same as multiplying by 10. Multiply 5.281 by 10 mentally.

5.281 = ___52.81___ tenths

Check by dividing with a calculator.

5.281 ÷ 0.1 = | 52.81 |

EXAMPLE 3 A gram is one-thousandth of a kilogram. How many grams are in 32 kilograms?

32 = _____ thousandths

Dividing by 0.001 is the same as multiplying by 1000. Multiply 32 by 1000 mentally.

32 = ___32,000___ thousandths

Check the answer with a calculator. Divide 32 by a thousandth or 0.001.

32 ÷ 0.001 = | 32000. |

So, 32 kg = 32,000 g.

Compute the answer mentally. Then check by using a calculator.

1. 40.7 = ___4.07___ tens

2. 40.7 = _____ tenths

3. 40.7 = _____ hundreds

4. 2.84 = _____ hundredths

5. 2.84 = _____ tenths

6. 2.84 = _____ tens

7. 391.2 = _____ hundreds

8. 391.2 = _____ tens

9. 0.84 = _____ hundredths

10. 0.84 = _____ tenths

11. 3401 = _____ tenths

12. 450 = _____ thousands

Solve. Use the method shown above.

---

13. A centimeter is one-hundredth of a meter. How many centimeters are in 20 meters?

20 = ___2000___ hundredths

Answer _____

14. A millimeter is one-thousandth of a meter. How many millimeters are in 43.2 meters?

Answer _____

---

15. A milligram is one-thousandth of a gram. How many milligrams are in 3.7 grams?

Answer _____

16. A kilogram is one thousand grams. How many kilograms are in 734 grams?

Answer _____

PROBLEM SOLVING

Applications

Solve.

---

1. A passenger train has 14 coaches. The length of each coach is 59 ft. What is the total length of the train without the engine?

Answer _____

2. A bushel of potatoes weighs about 26 kilograms. What is the weight of 5225 bushels loaded into a boxcar for shipment?

Answer _____

---

3. The Garcias own a citrus grove. They pay $6.45 per acre each time they have it irrigated. If the grove contains 48 acres, what does it cost each time for irrigating?

Answer _____

4. John could jump about 6 times as high on the moon as he could on Earth. If he could jump 30.6 feet on the moon how high could he jump on Earth?

Answer _____

---

5. An airliner carried 73 passengers from San Francisco to Chicago. The fare was $153.48. How much money was received by the airline for that flight?

Answer _____

6. An agriculture class raised 2535 bushels of potatoes on 39 acres. What was the average yield per acre?

Answer _____

---

7. Mrs. George made one payment of $37.50 and one payment of $73.94. How much did she pay in all?

Answer _____

8. A jet plane made a flight of 6510 miles in 15.5 hours. What average speed did it make?

Answer _____

Metric Measurement

The basic metric units are meter (m), liter (L), and gram (g). These basic unit names are used with prefixes to form the names of larger and smaller units.

To change from one unit to another, find the unit in the chart below. Move to the new unit. When you move right to a smaller unit, multiply by 10 for each step. When you move left to a larger unit, divide by 10 for each step.

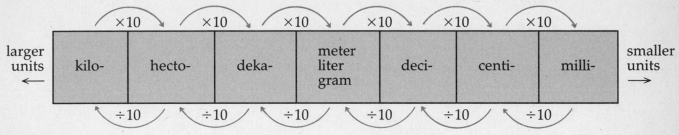

Find: 15 hm = _____ m

To change hm to m, find hecto in the table. Find meter in the table. To change hm to a smaller unit, multiply by 10 for each step.

15 hm = (15 × 10 × 10) m
= (15 × 100) m
15 hm = 1500 m

You will have more smaller units.

Find: 9000 mL = _____ L

To change mL to L, find milli in the table. Find liter in the table. To change mL to a larger unit, divide by 10 for each step.

9000 mL = (9000 ÷ 10 ÷ 10 ÷ 10) L
= (9000 ÷ 1000) L
9000 mL = 9 L

You will have fewer larger units.

Change each measurement to a smaller unit.

	a	b	c
1.	5 g = _____ mg	127 L = _____ dL	97 kg = _____ g
2.	46 cm = _____ mm	12 km = _____ m	8 L = _____ mL

Change each measurement to a larger unit.

	a	b	c
3.	48,000 L = _____ kL	980 mm = _____ cm	2100 mg = _____ g
4.	500 hg = _____ kg	17,000 m = _____ km	3000 g = _____ kg

PROBLEM-SOLVING STRATEGY

Identify Extra Information

Some problems contain information that is not needed to solve the problem. When you read a problem, it may be helpful to cross out the extra facts.

Read the problem.

> Everett typed a 500-word essay in 6 minutes 30 seconds. How many seconds did it take him to type the essay?

Decide which facts are needed.

> The problem asks for the number of seconds. You need to change 6 minutes to seconds, then add 30 seconds. Recall that there are 60 seconds in a minute.

Decide which facts are extra.

> You do not need to know that the essay has 500 words.

Solve the problem.

> Multiply the number of minutes by 60. Then add 30 seconds.
>
> Seconds in 6 minutes: $6 \times 60 = 360$ seconds
>
> Total seconds: $360 + 30 = 390$ seconds
>
> Everett typed the essay in 390 seconds.

In each problem, cross out the extra facts. Then solve the problem.

---

1. Oliver worked 8.5 hours on Monday, 6 hours on Tuesday, ~~and 7.5 hours on Wednesday.~~ How much longer did he work on Monday than Tuesday?

   Answer _____

2. Winona bought a car that cost $5480, including a $199 service warranty. She paid $1000 as a down payment and took out a loan for the rest. What was the amount of her loan?

   Answer _____

---

3. Ernest works part-time and earns $75 per week. If he saves about $25 per week, how much money will he save in 6 weeks?

   Answer _____

4. Iris spent $4.32 for a calculator, $12.89 for a backpack, and $8.99 for a lantern. How much more did the lantern cost than the calculator?

   Answer _____

In each problem, cross out the extra facts. Then solve the problem.

---

5. A ream of paper contains 500 sheets. If a person buys 12 reams for $5.25 each, what is the total cost?

Answer _____

6. A 16-inch pizza costs $11.95. If five friends share the cost equally, how much does each friend pay?

Answer _____

7. The original price of a jogging suit was $38.50. Tommy bought the suit on sale for $28.95. He also spent $6.29 for gloves. How much did Tommy spend for the jogging suit and gloves?

Answer _____

8. Martha is 63 inches tall and weighs 115 pounds. Her sister is 67 inches tall and weighs 122 pounds. How much shorter is Martha than her sister?

Answer _____

9. Rayleen paid $2.69 for an 8-foot strip of molding. If she cut off 2 feet 4 inches of molding, find the length of the remaining piece.

Answer _____

10. The distance from Greg's house to school is 4.2 kilometers. The distance to the library is 2.7 kilometers. If Greg rides his bike from home to school and back, how far does he ride?

Answer _____

11. Evelyn worked 4 hours 15 minutes before lunch, then took a break for 45 minutes. She worked 3 hours 30 minutes after lunch. How much time was she working that day?

Answer _____

12. Winnie works part-time and earns $44 per week. She earns $5.50 per hour. How much does she earn in 12 weeks?

Answer _____

13. Brad drove 134 miles in 2 hours 20 minutes. How many minutes did he drive?

Answer _____

14. A carton of milk contains 250 milliliters and costs 39¢. How many cartons could be filled from 4 liters of milk?

Answer _____

PROBLEM SOLVING

Applications

Solve.

1. Joe went to the grocery story and purchased meat for $2.48, butter for $1.88, tomatoes for $0.87, and canned goods for $3.89. How much did all of these cost?

Answer _____

2. Mr. Burt bought gas for the car at $9.75, oil for $0.70, a new tire for $48.75, and a filter for $5.15. What was the total bill?

Answer _____

3. Elida gave the storekeeper a twenty-dollar bill for a purchase of $14.51. How much change should she have received?

Answer _____

4. Marie bought 4 yards of material at $3.52 a yard. How much did she pay for the 4 yards?

Answer _____

5. Jorge bought 3 shirts at $18.49 each. How much did he pay for the 3 shirts?

Answer _____

6. Mrs. Turner paid $7.47 for a three-pound roast. What was the price per pound?

Answer _____

7. Mr. Parker drove 720 kilometers in 9 hours. What was his average rate of speed?

Answer _____

8. Josie bought five oranges for $1.15. At this price, how much would one orange cost?

Answer _____

REVIEWING BASIC SKILLS
Unit 1 Review

Add or subtract.

	a	b	c	d
1.	343 + 23	452.9 −342.8	55,234 − 2,566	$209.89 + 178.93
2.	78.3 + 0.23	3 −2.6	6271 −4286	276.0 + 15.9
3.	45,493 − 7,723	6264 +8740	6.234 −5.667	9.89 203.9 +648.9

Multiply or divide.

	a	b	c	d
4.	73 ×25	2.93 ×0.81	32,234 × 6	439.89 × 0.9

5.

a	b	c	d
8)8976	76)8.74	0.97)67,221	5.2)5428.8

Estimate.

	a	b	c
6.	65.90→ +553.6 →	38.5 −23	145 +765
7.	387 × 6	97)436	258 ×3.5

Change each measurement.

	a	b	c
8.	37 m = _____ cm	397 kg = _____ g	1.9 L = _____ mL

Fractions

Write the fraction for each word name.

	a	b	c
1.	two fifths _$\frac{2}{5}$_	one ninth _____	five sixtieths _____

Write the word name for each fraction.

	a	b	c
2.	$\frac{2}{3}$ _two thirds_	$\frac{7}{10}$ _____	$\frac{1}{88}$ _____

There are 12 eggs in a dozen. Each egg is $\frac{1}{12}$ dozen. Write the following as a fraction of a dozen. Write the word name for the fraction.

	a	b	c
3.	7 eggs = _$\frac{7}{12}$_ dozen	5 eggs = _____ dozen	11 eggs = _____ dozen
	seven twelfths		

Simplify.

	a	b	c	d
4.	$\frac{12}{18}$ = _$\frac{2}{3}$_	$\frac{3}{6}$ = _____	$\frac{10}{15}$ = _____	$\frac{8}{10}$ = _____
	$\frac{12 \div 6}{18 \div 6} = \frac{2}{3}$			
5.	$\frac{6}{6}$ = _____	$\frac{8}{16}$ = _____	$\frac{6}{9}$ = _____	$\frac{12}{14}$ = _____

Find the lowest common denominator (LCD) for each pair of fractions. Then rewrite each pair of fractions as equivalent fractions in higher terms.

	a	b	c	d
6.	$\frac{3}{4} = \frac{3 \times 5}{4 \times 5} = \frac{15}{20}$	$\frac{1}{2}$ =	$\frac{7}{10}$ =	$\frac{11}{12}$ =
	$\frac{1}{5} = \frac{1 \times 4}{5 \times 4} = \frac{4}{20}$	$\frac{2}{3}$ =	$\frac{2}{15}$ =	$\frac{5}{8}$ =

Mixed Numbers

Write as a mixed number or whole number. Simplify.

	a	*b*	*c*

1. $\frac{15}{15} =$ ____ 1 $15\overline{)15}$ $\frac{1}{}$ $\frac{6}{6} =$ _____ $\frac{9}{9} =$ _____

2. $\frac{27}{9} =$ _____ $\frac{32}{8} =$ _____ $\frac{36}{6} =$ _____

3. $\frac{37}{5} =$ ____ $7\frac{2}{5}$ $5\overline{)37}$ $7\frac{2}{5}$
    $\frac{3\ 5}{2}$
                                    $\frac{24}{10} =$ _____ $\frac{54}{7} =$ _____

4. $\frac{59}{8} =$ _____ $\frac{31}{8} =$ _____ $\frac{27}{4} =$ _____

5. $\frac{73}{9} =$ _____ $\frac{145}{16} =$ _____ $\frac{107}{9} =$ _____

Write as an improper fraction.

	a	*b*	*c*

6. $3 =$ ____ $\frac{3}{1}$ $7 =$ _____ $2 =$ _____

7. $5\frac{3}{5} =$ ____ $\frac{28}{5}$
    $5 \times 5 + 3 = 28$ $4\frac{2}{7} =$ _____ $14\frac{6}{11} =$ _____

8. $8\frac{2}{11} =$ _____ $24\frac{6}{7} =$ _____ $4\frac{3}{10} =$ _____

9. $1\frac{7}{9} =$ _____ $3\frac{1}{7} =$ _____ $15\frac{1}{5} =$ _____

10. $6\frac{2}{9} =$ _____ $5\frac{3}{7} =$ _____ $1\frac{5}{9} =$ _____

REVIEWING BASIC SKILLS
Customary Measurement

Some customary units of length are the inch, foot, yard, and mile. The chart shows the relationship of one unit to another.

1 foot (ft)	= 12 inches (in.)
1 yard (yd)	= 3 ft
	= 36 in.
1 mile (mi)	= 1760 yd
	= 5280 ft

Some customary units of weight are the ounce, pound, and ton. The chart shows the relationship of one unit to another.

1 pound (lb)	= 16 ounces (oz)
1 ton (T)	= 2000 pounds

Some customary units of capacity are the cup, pint, quart, and gallon. The chart shows the relationship of one unit to another.

1 pint (pt)	= 2 cups (c)
1 quart (qt)	= 2 pt
	= 4 c
1 gallon (gal)	= 4 qt
	= 8 pt
	= 16 c

Change each measurement to a larger unit.

	a	b
1.	98 in. = __8__ ft __2__ in.	37 in. = ____ ft ____ in.

$$\begin{array}{r} 8\ R\ 2 \\ 12\overline{)98} \\ \underline{96} \\ 2 \end{array}$$

	a	b
2.	28 oz = ____ lb ____ oz	64 oz = ____ lb ____ oz
3.	9 pt = ____ qt ____ pt	31 qt = ____ gal ____ qt

Change each measurement to a smaller unit.

	a	b	c
4.	2 yd = __72__ in.	15 ft = _____ in.	2 mi = _____ ft

$$2 \times 36 = 72$$

	a	b	c
5.	3 lb = _____ oz	20 lb = _____ oz	14 T = _____ lb
6.	8 qt 1 c = _____ c	10 pt = _____ c	4 gal = _____ pt

Addition of Fractions

Remember,
- to simplify a proper fraction, write it in simplest terms.
- to simplify an improper fraction, write it as a whole or mixed number.

Add. Simplify.

	a	b	c	d
1.	$\frac{4}{7}$ $+\frac{3}{7}$ $\frac{7}{7}=1$	$\frac{10}{13}$ $+\frac{4}{13}$	$\frac{2}{3}$ $+\frac{1}{3}$	$\frac{12}{17}$ $+\frac{1}{17}$
2.	$\frac{7}{11}=\frac{14}{22}$ $+\frac{4}{22}=\frac{4}{22}$ $\frac{18}{22}=\frac{9}{11}$	$\frac{2}{5}$ $+\frac{1}{3}$	$\frac{4}{8}$ $+\frac{1}{4}$	$\frac{8}{11}$ $+\frac{2}{9}$
3.	$\frac{6}{7}=\frac{12}{14}$ $+\frac{1}{2}=\frac{7}{14}$ $\frac{19}{14}=1\frac{5}{14}$	$\frac{3}{5}$ $+\frac{2}{3}$	$\frac{9}{12}$ $+\frac{3}{4}$	$\frac{1}{2}$ $+\frac{2}{3}$
4.	$\frac{5}{8}=\frac{15}{24}$ $+\frac{1}{3}=\frac{8}{24}$ $\frac{23}{24}$	$\frac{1}{4}$ $+\frac{1}{3}$	$\frac{5}{6}$ $+\frac{3}{4}$	$\frac{3}{5}$ $+\frac{2}{3}$

Line up the digits. Add and simplify.

	a	b	c
5.	$\frac{2}{7}+\frac{2}{6}=$ _____ $\frac{2}{7}$ $+\frac{2}{6}$	$\frac{2}{3}+\frac{4}{5}=$ _____	$\frac{7}{9}+\frac{6}{8}=$ _____
6.	$\frac{4}{5}+\frac{2}{4}=$ _____	$\frac{3}{9}+\frac{9}{12}=$ _____	$\frac{7}{9}+\frac{2}{10}=$ _____

Addition of Mixed Numbers

Add. Simplify.

	a	*b*	*c*	*d*
1.	$4\frac{4}{12}$	$5\frac{3}{4}$	$3\frac{5}{6}$	$3\frac{9}{10}$
	$+\,3\frac{7}{12}$	$+\,1\frac{2}{4}$	$+\,7\frac{3}{6}$	$+\,1\frac{7}{10}$
	$7\frac{11}{12}$			

2. $8\frac{2}{6}=8\frac{4}{12}$	$7\frac{3}{5}$	$23\frac{2}{7}$	$13\frac{3}{8}$
$+\,3\frac{4}{12}=3\frac{4}{12}$	$+\,2\frac{5}{10}$	$+\,16\frac{1}{14}$	$+\,21\frac{3}{4}$
$11\frac{8}{12}=11\frac{2}{3}$			

3. $6\frac{8}{9}=6\frac{8}{9}$	$32\frac{4}{5}$	$4\frac{6}{8}$	$16\frac{4}{32}$
$+\,7\frac{2}{3}=7\frac{6}{9}$	$+\,14\frac{6}{15}$	$+\,25\frac{1}{2}$	$+\,34\frac{4}{8}$
$13\frac{14}{9}=14\frac{5}{9}$			

4. $3\frac{4}{5}=3\frac{16}{20}$	$14\frac{5}{6}$	$4\frac{2}{7}$	$14\frac{1}{3}$
$+\,2\frac{3}{4}=2\frac{15}{20}$	$+\,34\frac{8}{9}$	$+\,2\frac{1}{3}$	$+\,15\frac{6}{8}$
$5\frac{31}{20}=6\frac{11}{20}$			

5. $7\frac{2}{5}=7\frac{6}{15}$	$7\frac{2}{9}$	$5\frac{5}{6}$	$25\frac{5}{8}$
$+\,5\frac{1}{3}=5\frac{5}{15}$	$+\,3\frac{3}{5}$	$+\,6\frac{2}{8}$	$+\,67\frac{3}{5}$
$12\frac{11}{15}$			

Line up the digits. Add. Simplify.

a	*b*	*c*
6. $2\frac{3}{8}+7\frac{3}{5}=$ _____	$9\frac{8}{11}+3\frac{4}{9}=$ _____	$14\frac{2}{5}+16\frac{2}{3}=$ _____

$$2\frac{3}{8}$$

$$+\,7\frac{3}{5}$$

Subtraction of Fractions

Subtract. Simplify.

	a	b	c	d

1.

a

$\dfrac{11}{12}$
$-\dfrac{7}{12}$
$\dfrac{4}{12} = \dfrac{1}{3}$

b

$\dfrac{7}{9}$
$-\dfrac{5}{9}$

c

$\dfrac{11}{15}$
$-\dfrac{8}{15}$

d

$\dfrac{5}{8}$
$-\dfrac{3}{8}$

2.

$\dfrac{5}{6} = \dfrac{10}{12}$
$-\dfrac{7}{12} = \dfrac{7}{12}$
$\dfrac{3}{12} = \dfrac{1}{4}$

$\dfrac{7}{8}$
$-\dfrac{3}{16}$

$\dfrac{6}{7}$
$-\dfrac{3}{14}$

$\dfrac{3}{8}$
$-\dfrac{1}{4}$

3.

$\dfrac{7}{8} = \dfrac{7}{8}$
$-\dfrac{1}{2} = \dfrac{4}{8}$
$\dfrac{3}{8}$

$\dfrac{4}{5}$
$-\dfrac{4}{15}$

$\dfrac{8}{9}$
$-\dfrac{1}{3}$

$\dfrac{5}{6}$
$-\dfrac{1}{18}$

4.

$\dfrac{5}{7} = \dfrac{15}{21}$
$-\dfrac{1}{3} = \dfrac{7}{21}$
$\dfrac{8}{21}$

$\dfrac{7}{9}$
$-\dfrac{1}{5}$

$\dfrac{5}{6}$
$-\dfrac{1}{4}$

$\dfrac{5}{8}$
$-\dfrac{1}{6}$

5.

$\dfrac{4}{9} = \dfrac{20}{45}$
$-\dfrac{2}{5} = \dfrac{18}{45}$
$\dfrac{2}{45}$

$\dfrac{1}{2}$
$-\dfrac{2}{9}$

$\dfrac{5}{8}$
$-\dfrac{4}{7}$

$\dfrac{1}{2}$
$-\dfrac{2}{7}$

Line up the digits. Subtract. Simplify.

a

b

c

6. $\dfrac{9}{11} - \dfrac{2}{3} =$ _____

$\dfrac{3}{5} - \dfrac{1}{2} =$ _____

$\dfrac{8}{9} - \dfrac{3}{4} =$ _____

$\dfrac{9}{11}$
$-\dfrac{2}{3}$

REVIEWING BASIC SKILLS

Subtraction of Mixed Numbers

Subtract. Simplify.

	a	*b*	*c*	*d*
1.	$4 = 3\frac{12}{12}$ $-\ 3\frac{7}{12} = 3\frac{7}{12}$ $\frac{5}{12}$	7 $-\ 1\frac{5}{8}$	$3\,4$ $-\,1\,2\frac{4}{18}$	$2\,3$ $-\,1\,5\frac{3}{11}$
2.	$8\frac{1}{4} = 7\frac{5}{4}$ $-\ 6\frac{3}{4} = 6\frac{3}{4}$ $1\frac{2}{4} = 1\frac{1}{2}$	$9\frac{5}{6}$ $-\ 7\frac{1}{6}$	$3\frac{9}{10}$ $-\ 1\frac{7}{10}$	$6\frac{2}{7}$ $-\ 3\frac{4}{7}$
3.	$2\,3\frac{2}{9} = 23\frac{4}{18}$ $-\,1\,6\frac{1}{18} = 16\frac{1}{18}$ $7\frac{3}{18} = 7\frac{1}{6}$	$3\frac{5}{6}$ $-\ 2\frac{2}{3}$	$2\,7\frac{3}{8}$ $-\,1\,5\frac{1}{4}$	$7\frac{5}{6}$ $-\ 4\frac{1}{12}$
4.	$1\,0\frac{5}{7} = 10\frac{15}{21}$ $-\ 4\frac{2}{3} = 4\frac{14}{21}$ $6\frac{1}{21}$	$2\,4\frac{2}{6}$ $-\,1\,0\frac{4}{5}$	$1\,7\frac{5}{6}$ $-\,1\,2\frac{2}{3}$	$3\,6\frac{4}{5}$ $-\,3\,2\frac{1}{4}$
5.	$1\,6\frac{1}{6} = 16\frac{4}{24} = 15\frac{28}{24}$ $-\ 9\frac{3}{8} = 9\frac{9}{24} = 9\frac{9}{24}$ $6\frac{19}{24}$	$7\frac{5}{9}$ $-\ 4\frac{1}{6}$	$8\frac{2}{5}$ $-\ 5\frac{2}{3}$	$1\,4\frac{1}{4}$ $-\,1\,1\frac{3}{5}$

Line up the digits. Subtract. Simplify.

	a	*b*	*c*
6.	$13\frac{4}{9} - 7\frac{1}{2} = \underline{\hspace{2cm}}$	$9\frac{7}{8} - 4\frac{7}{8} = \underline{\hspace{2cm}}$	$24\frac{2}{5} - 16\frac{4}{5} = \underline{\hspace{2cm}}$

$13\frac{4}{9}$

$-\ 7\frac{1}{2}$

PROBLEM SOLVING

Applications

Solve.

1. Renee used $1\frac{1}{2}$ dozen eggs to make deviled eggs. Tony pickled $1\frac{3}{4}$ dozen eggs. How many dozen eggs did they use in all?

Answer _____

2. The Shins went on a trip. They traveled $\frac{1}{12}$ of the trip on the first day, and $\frac{5}{12}$ on the second day. How much more do they have to travel?

Answer _____

3. One recipe calls for $3\frac{3}{4}$ cups of flour. Another recipe uses $2\frac{1}{3}$ cups of flour. What is the difference in the amounts of flour?

Answer _____

4. Quinn bought $3\frac{3}{4}$ pounds of cheese and $5\frac{5}{8}$ fish at the store. How many pounds of food did he buy in all?

Answer _____

5. Sam is $5\frac{2}{7}$ feet tall. How much would he have to grow to be 6 feet tall?

Answer _____

6. Enrico mailed 2 packages. One weighed $4\frac{2}{5}$ pounds and the other weighed $5\frac{4}{5}$ pounds. How much did the packages weigh in all?

Answer _____

7. Sable spent $3\frac{1}{4}$ hours reading a book, $1\frac{7}{8}$ hours doing homework, and 1 hour playing a game. How many hours did she spend doing these activities?

Answer _____

8. Raj walks $\frac{3}{8}$ mile to school. Kevin walks $\frac{1}{4}$ mile to get to school. Who walks the furthest distance? By how much?

Answer _____

31

PROBLEM-SOLVING STRATEGY

Make a Table

For some problems, it is necessary to make many calculations before finding the final answer. It is easier to solve this type of problem if the information is organized in a table.

Read the problem.

> An art supply store sells markers for 40¢ each and sketch pads for 70¢ each. How many of each can you buy for exactly $3.40?

Make a table.

> Calculate the price of different combinations of markers and sketch pads. Organize the results in a table. For example, here is how to find the cost of 3 markers and 2 sketch pads.
>
> $$(3 \times \$0.40) + (2 \times \$0.70) = \$1.20 + \$1.40$$
> $$= \$2.60$$

Number of markers

	0	1	2	3	4	5
0	$0	$0.40	$0.80	$1.20	$1.60	$2.00
1	$0.70	$1.10	$1.50			
2	$1.40			$2.60	$3.00	$3.40
3	$2.10			$3.30	$3.70	
4	$2.80	$3.20	$3.60			
5	$3.50					

Number of Sketch Pads

Solve the problem.

> The table shows that you can get 5 markers and 2 sketch pads for exactly $3.40.

Solve.

1. Complete the table shown above.

2. Eric spent exactly $2.50 for markers and sketch pads at the art supply store. Use the table to find out the number of sketch pads that he bought. (Hint: Use the table above.)

3. Lauren spent exactly $4.10 for markers and sketch pads at the art supply store. Use the table to find out the number of markers that she bought. (Hint: Use the table above.)

Answer _____

Answer _____

Solve.

4. A store sells containers of fruit yogurt for $0.65 and plain yogurt for $0.50. Complete the table at the right to show the combinations.

	Plain Yogurt			
Fruit Yogurt	0	1	2	3
0	$0	$0.50		
1	$0.65			
2				
3				

5. Mitch spent $3.45. How many of each type did he buy? (Hint: Use your completed table.)

Answer _____

6. Lisa spent $1.80. How many of each type did she buy? (Hint: Use your completed table.)

Answer _____

7. Carl emptied 25 pennies and dimes from his pockets. He had $1.33 in all. How many pennies did he have in his pockets?

Dimes	Pennies	Total Value	
3	22	$2.23	No

Answer _____

8. Gretchen has 10 coins in her purse with a total value of $1.60. The coins are dimes and quarters. How many of each coin does she have?

Quarters	Dimes	Total Value	
1	9	$1.15	No

Answer _____

9. Minnie can spend exactly 50¢ for some of these items.

    Rulers, 5¢ each

    Pencils, 10¢ each

    Folders, 25¢ each

What can she buy? Use the table to show all the possibilities.

Folders 25¢	Pencils 10¢	Rulers 5¢	Total

Multiplication of Fractions

Multiply. Simplify.

	a	*b*	*c*	*d*
1.	$\frac{3}{5} \times \frac{2}{5} = \frac{6}{25}$	$\frac{5}{9} \times \frac{7}{9} =$	$\frac{3}{8} \times \frac{7}{8} =$	$\frac{6}{7} \times \frac{3}{7} =$

2. $\frac{3}{7} \times \frac{8}{9} = \frac{8}{21}$ $\quad\quad$ $\frac{2}{5} \times \frac{7}{8} =$ $\quad\quad$ $\frac{6}{7} \times \frac{2}{3} =$ $\quad\quad$ $\frac{6}{7} \times \frac{3}{5} =$

$\frac{1\cancel{3}}{7} \times \frac{8}{\cancel{9}_3} = \frac{8}{21}$

3. $8 \times \frac{2}{5} = 3\frac{1}{5}$ $\quad\quad$ $\frac{1}{9} \times 6 =$ $\quad\quad$ $5 \times \frac{6}{7} =$ $\quad\quad$ $\frac{3}{4} \times 2 =$

$\frac{8}{1} \times \frac{2}{5} = \frac{16}{5} = 3\frac{1}{5}$

4. $4\frac{2}{7} \times \frac{4}{5} = 3\frac{3}{7}$ $\quad\quad$ $\frac{7}{9} \times 3\frac{4}{5} =$ $\quad\quad$ $6 \times 8\frac{5}{8} =$ $\quad\quad$ $7\frac{1}{8} \times 8 =$

$\frac{^6\cancel{30}}{7} \times \frac{4}{\cancel{5}_1} = \frac{24}{7} = 3\frac{3}{7}$

5. $4\frac{4}{8} \times 8\frac{8}{9} = 40$ $\quad\quad$ $3\frac{2}{5} \times 16\frac{2}{7} =$ $\quad\quad$ $3\frac{1}{9} \times 7\frac{3}{4} =$ $\quad\quad$ $9\frac{1}{16} \times 4\frac{1}{2} =$

$\frac{^4\cancel{36}}{1\cancel{8}} \times \frac{\cancel{80}^{10}}{\cancel{9}_1} = \frac{40}{1} = 40$

Multiply. Simplify.

	a	*b*	*c*
6.	$\frac{8}{9} \times \frac{7}{8} \times \frac{4}{7} = \frac{4}{9}$	$\frac{5}{6} \times \frac{1}{9} \times \frac{9}{15} =$	$\frac{2}{5} \times \frac{1}{8} \times \frac{4}{7} =$

$\frac{1\cancel{8}}{9} \times \frac{1\cancel{7}}{\cancel{8}_1} \times \frac{4}{\cancel{7}_1} = \frac{4}{9}$

Division of Fractions

Remember, to divide by a fraction, multiply by its reciprocal.

Divide. Simplify.

	a	*b*	*c*	*d*
1.	$\frac{2}{5} \div \frac{3}{5} = \frac{2}{3}$	$\frac{7}{8} \div \frac{7}{8} =$	$\frac{8}{9} \div \frac{4}{9} =$	$\frac{5}{6} \div \frac{1}{6} =$

$\frac{2}{5} \times \frac{5}{3} = \frac{2}{3}$

2.	$\frac{3}{7} \div \frac{5}{9} = \frac{27}{35}$	$\frac{5}{6} \div \frac{1}{8} =$	$\frac{2}{7} \div \frac{1}{3} =$	$\frac{3}{16} \div \frac{3}{8} =$

$\frac{3}{7} \times \frac{9}{5} = \frac{27}{35}$

3.	$2 \div \frac{5}{6} = 2\frac{2}{5}$	$\frac{8}{9} \div 5 =$	$3 \div \frac{3}{5} =$	$\frac{1}{2} \div 4 =$

$\frac{2}{1} \times \frac{6}{5} = \frac{12}{5} = 2\frac{2}{5}$

4.	$4 \div 2\frac{7}{11} - 1\frac{15}{29}$	$5\frac{3}{4} \div 3 =$	$7 \div 8\frac{1}{3} =$	$3\frac{2}{3} \div 8 -$

$\frac{4}{1} \times \frac{11}{29} = \frac{44}{29} = 1\frac{15}{29}$

5.	$3\frac{3}{4} \div \frac{2}{5} = 9\frac{3}{8}$	$\frac{3}{13} \div 4\frac{4}{26} =$	$5\frac{2}{5} \div \frac{4}{5} =$	$\frac{3}{8} \div 8\frac{7}{16} =$

$\frac{15}{4} \times \frac{5}{2} = \frac{75}{8} = 9\frac{3}{8}$

6.	$3\frac{4}{9} \div 2\frac{1}{8} = 1\frac{95}{123}$	$8\frac{1}{6} \div 5\frac{7}{8} =$	$4\frac{2}{5} \div 6\frac{3}{5} =$	$2\frac{5}{8} \div 8\frac{3}{4} =$

$\frac{31}{9} \times \frac{8}{17} = \frac{248}{123} = 1\frac{95}{123}$

Meaning of Percent

The symbol % is read as *percent*. Percent means *per hundred* or *out of one hundred*. Therefore, 78% means 78 per hundred or 78 out of 100, or 78 hundredths.

By writing the percent as hundredths, we can write a percent as a fraction or as a decimal.

To change a *percent to a decimal,* move the decimal point 2 places to the left and drop the percent sign (%). Write zeros as needed.

EXAMPLES

$$78\% = 0.78 \qquad 001\% = 0.01 \qquad 200\% = 2.00$$

To change a *percent to a fraction,* place the percent over 100 and drop the % sign. Simplify.

EXAMPLES

$$78\% = \frac{78}{100} = \frac{39}{50} \qquad 1\% = \frac{1}{100} \qquad 200\% = \frac{200}{100} = 2$$

PRACTICE

Change each percent to a decimal and then to a fraction. Simplify.

	a	*b*
1.	32% = _____	5% = _____
2.	4% = _____	95% = _____
3.	21% = _____	60% = _____
4.	1% = _____	300% = _____
5.	100% = _____	7% = _____
6.	15% = _____	3% = _____
7.	89% = _____	75% = _____
8.	90% = _____	42% = _____

Changing Decimals and Fractions to Percents

To change a *decimal to a percent*, move the decimal point 2 places to the right and write a percent symbol. Write zeros as needed.

EXAMPLES

$0.264 = 26.4\%$ $0.05 = 5\%$ $0.80 = 80\%$

PRACTICE

Change the following to percents.

	a	b	c
1.	$0.19 = $ __19%__	$0.30 = $ _____	$0.65 = $ _____
2.	$0.01 = $ _____	$0.1 = $ _____	$0.90 = $ _____
3.	$0.75 = $ _____	$0.18 = $ _____	$0.09 = $ _____
4.	$0.05 = $ _____	$0.183 = $ _____	$0.2 = $ _____
5.	$0.10 = $ _____	$0.6 = $ _____	$0.41 = $ _____

To change a *fraction to a percent*, first change the fraction to a decimal by dividing the numerator by the denominator. Then rewrite the decimal quotient as a percent.

Write $\frac{4}{5}$ as a percent.

Divide.
$$\frac{0.80}{5\overline{)4.00}} = 80\%$$

Write $\frac{1}{8}$ as a percent.

Divide.
$$\frac{0.125}{8\overline{)1.000}} = 12.5\% = 12\frac{1}{2}\%$$

PRACTICE

Change the following to percents.

	a	b	c
6.	$\frac{1}{5} = $ __20%__	$\frac{9}{10} = $ _____	$\frac{1}{2} = $ _____
7.	$\frac{7}{10} = $ _____	$\frac{3}{4} = $ _____	$\frac{1}{4} = $ _____
8.	$\frac{1}{16} = $ _____	$\frac{3}{8} = $ _____	$\frac{2}{16} = $ _____

Interchanging Fractions, Decimals, and Percents

Fill in the blanks below as illustrated in the first example.

-Work Space-

1. $\dfrac{1}{10}$ = _____0.10_____ = _____10%_____

2. $\dfrac{1}{2}$ = _____ = _____

3. _____ = 0.75 = _____

4. _____ = 0.30 = _____

5. _____ = _____ = 45%

6. _____ = _____ = 20%

Solve.

7. Computer sales are up $26\frac{1}{2}\%$. Write $26\frac{1}{2}\%$ as a decimal.

    Answer _____

8. Thomas spends twenty percent of his salary for food. What fraction of his income does he spend on food?

    Answer _____

9. Janet told her class that 18 of the 20 varieties of flowers she planted have bloomed. What percent of Janet's flowers have bloomed?

    Answer _____

10. Some city and state sales taxes total 6%. Write the decimal a salesclerk would use to find the tax on a purchase.

    Answer _____

11. Fifty percent of the Record Club members attended the last meeting. Write fifty percent as a fraction.

    Answer _____

12. In the U.S., two out of five families have more than one car. Write this fraction as a decimal.

    Answer _____

Percents Greater Than 100% and Less Than 1%

Large percents are used just like the small percents we have been using. Proceed as you did with small percents. To change the percent to a decimal, move the decimal point 2 places to the left. Drop the percent sign.

EXAMPLES

$100\% = 1.00 = 1$ $225\% = 2.25$ $142\frac{1}{2}\% = 142.5\% = 1.425$

PRACTICE

Change each percent to a decimal.

	a	b	c
1.	$600\% = $ _____ 6	$250\frac{1}{2}\% = $ _____	$275\% = $ _____
2.	$225\% = $ _____	$125\% = $ _____	$187\frac{1}{2} = $ _____
3.	$101\% = $ _____	$300\% = $ _____	$199\% = $ _____

To solve problems using percents smaller than 1%, change the fraction to a decimal.

EXAMPLES

$1\% = \frac{1}{100} = 100 \overline{)1.00}^{\,0.01}$ $\frac{1}{2}\% = 0.5\% = \frac{0.5}{100} = 100 \overline{)0.500}^{\,0.005}$

PRACTICE

Change each percent to a decimal.

	a	b	c
4.	$\frac{1}{4}\% = $ _____ 0.0025	$\frac{2}{5}\% = $ _____	$\frac{1}{10}\% = $ _____
5.	$\frac{5}{16}\% = $ _____	$\frac{5}{8}\% = $ _____	$\frac{4}{5}\% = $ _____
6.	$\frac{1}{8}\% = $ _____	$\frac{3}{4}\% = $ _____	$\frac{3}{10}\% = $ _____

Finding a Percent of a Number

To find a percent of a number, write a percent sentence. Every percent sentence consists of three numbers: the rate, the whole, and the part.

$$15\% \text{ of } 80 = 12$$

rate   whole   part

If the **part** is missing in a percent problem, solve by first changing the *rate* to a decimal. Then multiply the rate by the *whole*.

Remember, "of" means multiply.

Find: 38% of 70

$$38\% \times 70 = ?$$
$$0.38 \times 70 = 26.6$$

Find: 4% of 57

$$4\% \times 57 = ?$$
$$0.04 \times 57 = 2.28$$

PRACTICE

Change each percent to a decimal. Solve.

	a	*b*
1.	15% of 60	5% of 400

$$15\% \times 60 =$$
$$0.15 \times 60 = 9$$

2.	28% of 120	20% of 60
3.	14% of 500	6% of 150
4.	8% of 80	35% of 200

5. Yolanda gets a 15% discount on purchases at the store where she works. What will her discount be on a purchase of $37.80?

6. State and city sales tax amounts to 6%. How much tax will Marty pay on the purchase of a watch costing $58.50?

Answer _____

Answer _____

Finding a Percent of a Number

Another way to find the missing *part* in a percent problem is to use fractions rather than decimals. Change the *rate* to a fraction. Multiply the fraction by the *whole*.

Find: 20% of 35

$$20\% = 0.20 = \frac{1}{5}$$
$$\frac{1}{5} \times 35 = 7$$

Find: 75% of 16

$$75\% = 0.75 = \frac{3}{4}$$
$$\frac{3}{4} \times 16 = 12$$

PRACTICE

Change each percent to a fraction. Solve.

	a	*b*
1.	50% of 60	25% of 400
2.	75% of 120	$33\frac{1}{3}\%$ of 45
3.	10% of 180	20% of 60
4.	40% of 150	60% of 160

5. During a 40%-off sale, Tina bought a dress which normally sold for $42.60. How much did she save by buying the dress while it was on sale?

6. Leonard set aside 20% of his salary for insurance and savings. If he earned $16,000, how much did he set aside?

Answer _____

Answer _____

41

Finding a Number When a Percent of It Is Known

To find the *whole* in a percent problem, write a percent sentence. Change
the *rate* to a decimal. Divide the *part* by the decimal.

35% of what number is 70?

$$35\% \text{ of } ? = 70$$
$$? = 70 \div 0.35$$
$$200 = 70 \div 0.35$$

25% of what number is 60?

$$25\% \text{ of } ? = 60$$
$$? = 60 \div 0.25$$
$$240 = 60 \div 0.25$$

PRACTICE

Change each percent to a decimal. Solve.

a *b*

1. 25% of what number is 10?

$$25\% \text{ of } ? = 10$$
$$? = 10 \div 0.25$$
$$40 = 10 \div 0.25$$

40% of what number is 100?

2. 10% of what number is 1.7?

200% of what number is 10?

3. 150% of what number is 150?

20% of what number is 60?

4. 25% of what number is 20?

2% of what number is 40?

5. 60% of what number is 9?

80% of what number is 4?

6. 25% of what number is 40?

100% of what number is 15?

Finding What Percent One Number Is of Another

To find the *rate* in a percent problem, write a percent sentence. Divide the *part* by the *whole*. Then write the decimal answer as a percent.

What percent of 30 is 24?

$$?\% \times 30 = 24$$
$$? = 24 \div 30$$
$$0.8 = 24 \div 30$$
$$0.8 = 80\%$$

What percent of 60 is 15?

$$?\% \times 60 = 15$$
$$? = 15 \div 60$$
$$0.25 = 15 \div 60$$
$$0.25 = 25\%$$

PRACTICE

Find the rate.

	a	*b*
1.	What percent of 64 is 16?	What percent of 28 is 14?

$$?\% \times 64 = 16$$
$$? = 16 \div 64$$
$$0.25 = 16 \div 64$$
$$0.25 = 25\%$$

2. What percent of 700 is 14?   What percent of 100 is 9?

3. What percent of 90 is 30?   What percent of 85 is 17?

4. What percent of 500 is 5?   What percent of 202 is 101?

5. What percent of 6000 is 600?   What percent of 500 is 50?

6. What percent of 184 is 92?   What percent of 100 is 1?

Percent of Decrease

To find the current value or amount, first multiply the original amount by the percent of decrease. Then subtract.

EXAMPLE   Bill bought a car last year for $7000. When he tried to sell it this year, he found the value of the car had decreased 20%. What is the current value of the car?

original value	→	*$7000*
percent of decrease	→	× *0.20*
amount of decrease	→	*$1400*

original value	→	*$7000*
amount of decrease	→	− *1400*
current value	→	*$5600*

Solve.

1. A storekeeper decreased the price of a coat by 20%. If the coat had been $45, what was the sale price?

   Answer _____

2. 660 people attended the opening basketball game. The attendance dropped 25% for the second game. How many people attended the second game?

   Answer _____

3. Last month the Brown family's electric bill was $68. This month their bill decreased by 12%. How much was their bill?

   Answer _____

4. Last year, the track team had 48 members. This year the membership dropped by 25%. How many people are on the track team this year?

   Answer _____

5. Last year, Jenny hit 15 home runs. This year her number of home runs decreased by 20%. How many home runs did Jenny hit this year?

   Answer _____

6. Joseph's TV shop reduced the price of their best-selling television by 30%. The television normally sells for $800. What is the new price of the television?

   Answer _____

REVIEWING BASIC SKILLS

Percent of Increase

To find the current value or amount, first multiply the original amount by the percent of increase. Then add.

EXAMPLE   Terri raised 3200 bushels of oats last year. Because of better weather conditions this year, she expects to increase her crop by 25%. How many bushels does she expect this year?

original value   → 3200 bu   original amount   → 3200 bu
percent of increase → ×0.25   amount of increase → + 800 bu
amount of increase → ‾‾‾‾‾‾‾   amount expected   → ‾‾‾‾‾‾‾
                          800 bu   4000 bu

Solve.

1. Last year a certain vacant lot cost $80,000. This year it will cost 10% more. How much will the lot cost this year?

   Answer _____

2. Laura earns $56.40 a day. If she gets a 10% raise, how much will she be earning?

   Answer _____

3. The number of employees at Harbor Construction rose by 16% between 1989 and 1990. In 1989, 25 people worked for Harbor Construction. How many people worked there in 1990?

   Answer _____

4. Last year, the Delaneys' monthly rent was $320. This year the rent was increased by 15%. What is the Delaneys' rent now?

   Answer _____

5. Lyle could type 50 words per minute on his first typing test. He increased this number by 14% on the second test. How many words per minute did Lyle type on the second test?

   Answer _____

6. After a brisk walk, Brenda's pulse rate rose by 10%. Her pulse rate was 70 beats per minute before the walk. What was her pulse rate after the walk?

   Answer _____

PROBLEM-SOLVING STRATEGY
Write a Number Sentence

A number sentence shows how numbers are related to each other. If one of the numbers is not known, write n instead of a number. To solve the number sentence, you may need to find a missing addend or missing factor. Study these examples.

EXAMPLE 1

Read the problem.

Sam combined some wheat flour and $2\frac{1}{4}$ cups of rye flour for a recipe. He used a total of 6 cups of flour. How much wheat flour did he use?

Write a number sentence.

In the number sentence, n is the unknown amount of wheat flour.

Wheat flour		Rye flour		Total flour
n	+	$2\frac{1}{4}$	=	6

Solve the problem.

To find n, the missing addend, subtract $2\frac{1}{4}$ from 6.

$$n = 6 - 2\frac{1}{4} = 3\frac{3}{4}$$

Since $3\frac{3}{4} + 2\frac{1}{4} = 6$, the amount of wheat flour is $3\frac{3}{4}$ cups.

EXAMPLE 2

Read the problem.

Fifty-five percent of the people at a meeting are wearing sneakers. If 11 people are wearing sneakers, how many people are at the meeting?

Write a number sentence.

In the number sentence, n is the number of people at the meeting. Write 55% as the decimal 0.55.

Percent		People at meeting		Number wearing sneakers
0.55	×	n	=	11

Solve the problem.

To find the missing factor, divide 11 by 0.55.

$$n = 11 \div 0.55 = 20$$

Since $0.55 \times 20 = 11$, the number of people at the meeting was 20.

Write a number sentence. Then solve the problem.

1. Molly Martin got a raise of 73¢ per hour. She now earns $9.38 per hour. What was her hourly rate before her raise?

   Number Sentence _____

   Answer _____

2. Twenty percent of the students in a class are wearing blue pants. If 10 students are wearing blue pants, how many students are in the class?

   Number Sentence _____

   Answer _____

3. A recipe calls for $\frac{3}{4}$ cups of margarine. If the recipe is tripled, how much margarine will be needed?

   Number Sentence _____

   Answer _____

4. This week, Bernie plans to work 24 hours. This is $\frac{2}{3}$ as many hours as he worked last week. How many hours did he work last week?

   Number Sentence _____

   Answer _____

5. Gary has jogged $1\frac{5}{8}$ miles along a hiking path that has a total length of $2\frac{1}{4}$ miles. If he wants to jog the entire path, how much farther does he have to jog?

   Number Sentence _____

   Answer _____

6. For a project, Ellen cut a long dowel rod into five equal pieces, each $4\frac{1}{2}$ inches long. What was the length of the dowel rod?

   Number Sentence _____

   Answer _____

7. One-tenth of the students in Mr. Albert's class had perfect attendance. If 3 students had perfect attendance, how many students are in the class?

   Number Sentence _____

   Answer _____

8. The length of a picture frame is 1.5 times the width. If the length is 24 inches, what is the width?

   Number Sentence _____

   Answer _____

REVIEWING BASIC SKILLS

Calculator Applications

A calculator can be used to do problems with percents. Some calculators have a percent key, %. However, it is just as easy to find percents without a percent key.

EXAMPLE 1   Of the 22 students in Jackie's math class, 7 students have red hair. What percent of the students have red hair? Round to the nearest percent.

Write a percent sentence: What percent of 22 is 7?

$? \times 22 = 7$ Divide: 7 $\div$ 22 $=$ | 0.3181818 |

To round the display to the nearest percent, first copy the digits over to the hundredths place (0.31). Then increase the hundredths digit by 1 if the thousandths digit is 5 or greater. So, this display rounds to 0.32 or 32%. So, 32% of the students in the class have red hair.

EXAMPLE 2   Of the 23 students in Jackie's math class, 35% have black hair. How many students have black hair?

Write a percent sentence: 35% of 23 is what number?

$0.35 \times 23 = ?$ Multiply: 23 $\times$ 0.35 $=$ | 8.05 |

Round 8.05 to a whole number. The number of students who have black hair is 8.

Round the number in each display to the nearest percent.

1. | 0.7941176 |

 _____79%_____

2. | 0.3548387 |

 _____

3. | 0.0489514 |

 _____

4. | 0.2222222 |

 _____

Solve. Round to the nearest whole number or percent.

5. In a class of 28 students, 5 were absent last Monday. What percent were absent?

Answer _____

6. In a school of 344 students, 326 students were present last Tuesday. What percent were present?

Answer _____

7. Mr. Ritter's class has 34 students. Seventeen percent of the students have blonde hair. How many have blonde hair?

Answer _____

8. Mrs. Norton's class has 29 students. If 41% of the students are wearing sweaters, how many are wearing sweaters?

Answer _____

Unit 2 Review

Change each measurement.

	a	b	c
1.	6 lb = _____ oz	52 in. = _____ ft _____ in.	15 pt = _____ c
2.	6 pt 3 c = _____ c	19 oz = _____ lb _____ oz	5 yd = _____ ft

Find each answer. Simplify.

	a	b	c	d
3.	$\frac{4}{5} - \frac{7}{10} =$ _____	$\frac{9}{10} \times \frac{1}{3} =$ _____	$\frac{2}{3} + \frac{7}{9} =$ _____	$\frac{4}{7} \div \frac{3}{14} =$ _____
4.	$2\frac{6}{7} \div 4\frac{3}{5} =$ _____	$8\frac{1}{8} - 6 =$ _____	$\frac{5}{6} \times \frac{3}{4} =$ _____	$4\frac{2}{3} + 5\frac{4}{9} =$ _____
5.	$\frac{7}{8} + \frac{3}{4} =$ _____	$2\frac{5}{6} \times 5\frac{6}{7} =$ _____	$9\frac{1}{4} - 3\frac{3}{8} =$ _____	$\frac{1}{4} \div \frac{3}{16} =$ _____

Find each number.

	a	b
6.	Find 8% of 96.	What is 15% of 350?
7.	What percent of 32 is 0.8?	What percent of 80 is 24?
8.	What is 56% of 240?	5% of what number is 65?
9.	9% of what number is 45?	Find 42% of 98.

EARNING MONEY
Hourly Wages

An **employee** is any person who earns money, or **wages,** to do work for another person or company. The **employer** is the person or company who pays the employee.

Some employees are paid an hourly wage. To find the total wages for a week, find the number of hours worked and multiply by the hourly wage.

EXAMPLE Carol is a cashier at Garden Records. She earns $6.50 per hour. She works from 1:00 P.M.-7:00 P.M. Tuesdays through Saturdays. How much does Carol earn per week?

Hours per day		Days per week		Hours per week
6	×	5	=	30

Total hours		Hourly wage		Pay per week
30	×	$6.50	=	$195.00

Carol earns $195.00 per week.

Find each person's weekly earnings. The hourly wage and the hours worked each day are listed in the chart.

	Name	Mon.	Tues.	Wed.	Thur.	Fri.	Sat.	Hours Worked	Hourly Wages	Weekly Earnings
1.	Louis Brandeis	8	8	8	8	8	0		$6.72	
2.	Elinor Woodward	7.5	7.5	4	7.5	7.5	4		$8.48	
3.	Norman Pucinski	0	8	8	5.5	8	8		$5.20	
4.	Thelma Watkins	6	7.5	7	8	6	0		$7.33	

5. James is a welder who earns $12.50 per hour. He works 8 hours per day, Monday through Friday. How much does James earn in one week?

Answer _____

6. Anna is an installer for the telephone company. She earns $13.10 per hour. How much does she earn in 37.5 hours?

Answer _____

7. Ted works in a paper-box factory. He receives $321.60 a week for 40 hours of work. Find his hourly wage.

Answer _____

8. Yvonne's hourly wage is raised from $11.09 per hour to $12.35 per hour. She works 40 hours per week. How much more does she earn per week at the new rate?

Answer _____

Hourly Wages: Overtime

Many employers pay a higher hourly wage for overtime work. Suppose an employee normally earns $6.30 per hour and works 40 hours per week. One week, the employee worked 48 hours and got overtime pay for the 8 extra hours, at 1.5 times the usual rate. How much will the employee earn for each hour of overtime?

$6.30 × 1.5 = $9.45   The overtime rate is $9.45 per hour.

Find the employees' total wages for the week.

Regular earnings   40 × $6.30 = $252.00
Overtime earnings   8 × $9.45 = $75.60
Total earnings $327.60

The employees' total earnings for the week were $327.60.

Suppose that overtime pays time-and-a-half. That is, the hourly wage for overtime is 1.5 times the regular hourly wage. Find the hourly wage for overtime, given the regular hourly wage.

1. $8.20   **2.** $5.86   **3.** $12.66   **4.** $7.65

_____   _____   _____   _____

Complete the chart to find the total weekly earnings for each employee. The overtime rate is time-and-a-half. Round each amount to the nearest cent.

	Job	Hourly Wage	Regular Hours	Regular Earnings	Overtime Hours	Overtime Rate	Overtime Earnings	Total Earnings
5.	Printer	$10.30	40		6			
6.	Food server	$5.50	40		4.5			
7.	Carpenter	$14.88	40		10			
8.	Retail clerk	$8.95	40		2.5			

9. Rita Higgins is a nurse. Her regular rate is $14.62 per hour. She is paid double-time (two times the hourly rate) for holidays. During one week, she worked 36 regular hours plus 8 holiday hours. Find her total earnings for the week.

Answer _____

EARNING MONEY

Salary

Some employees earn a **salary,** or fixed amount, during each pay period. Suppose an employee's salary is $19,700 per year. What is the weekly salary? Divide by the number of weeks in a year.

Salary per year	Weeks per year	Salary per week
$19,700 ÷	52 =	$378.85

Complete the chart. Round amounts to the nearest cent. (Hint: Find the monthly salary by dividing the yearly salary by 12.)

	Job	Weekly Salary	Yearly Salary	Monthly Salary
1.	Store Manager	$653.95		
2.	Librarian		$38,420.20	
3.	Dietician	$363.46		
4.	Biologist		$25,200.00	
5.	Drafter	$410.00		

6. Linda earns $2538 per month. Billie earns $32,700 per year. Who earns more, Linda or Billie?

Answer _____

7. Phyllis earns a salary of $1830 per month. If she gets an 7% raise, how much more will she earn each month?

Answer _____

8. Karl's salary is $30,500 per year. If he gets a 10% raise, what will his yearly salary be?

Answer _____

9. Rodney's salary was raised $80 per week. What was his yearly increase?

Answer _____

10. Ted sets aside 8% of his monthly salary of $2800 for retirement. Mary saves $50 a week from her salary. Who saves more in one year?

Answer _____

11. An employee earns $1243 per month. What is the weekly salary? (Hint: Find the yearly salary before you find the weekly salary.)

Answer _____

EARNING MONEY

Wages and Tips

Workers in many service jobs earn tips from customers. Most waiters, taxi drivers, hair stylists, delivery drivers, and bellhops earn tips in addition to their hourly wage, which may be very low. By law, employees that earn tips regularly in their job must report the amount of tips to the employer. This is necessary because employees are required to pay taxes on this income as well as regular wages.

EXAMPLE   Ruben Altaha is a waiter in a restaurant. He works about 7 hours each day at $2.10 per hour. On an average day he earns about $45 in tips. About how much does he earn in wages and tips each day? About how much does he earn per week if he works 5 days?

Wages ($2.10 × 7)	+	Tips $45	=	Total per day $59.70

Total per day $60	×	Days per week 5	=	Weekly earnings $300

Including tips, Ruben earns about $60 per day or $300 per week.

Solve.

1. A hair stylist at Pierre's hair salon earns $6.80 per hour plus tips. The stylist works 40 hours per week with tips of about $240 per week. Find the total weekly earnings.

   Answer _____

2. Jerry is a parking lot attendant. He earns $2.50 per hour plus tips of about $8 per hour. About how much does he earn in a 40-hour week?

   Answer _____

3. Helen is a waitress in Mama Lucia's Cafe. She earns $32 per day in wages, and her tips average $3 per table. Helen serves about 20 tables each day. Including tips, about how much does she earn per day?

   Answer _____

4. Stella works as a manicurist. She works five 8-hour days per week, earning $4.50 per hour plus tips. On the average, she gets $15 per day in tips. Including tips, about how much does she earn each week?

   Answer _____

5. Angelo delivers pizzas. He is paid $7.20 per hour plus tips. Here are the amounts earned from tips one week: Monday $22, Tuesday $30, Wednesday $27, Friday $23, Saturday, $32. Find his total earnings for that week if he worked 40 hours.

   Answer _____

6. Tahshi works part-time as a bellhop at a hotel. She earns $3.75 per hour and works 20 hours per week. Here are the amounts of her tips one week: $9, $8.50, $12.25, $15.75. Including tips, about how much does she earn per week?

   Answer _____

EARNING MONEY

Commission

Commission is a fee on a percentage basis for work done. Many persons, especially salespersons, work on commission alone or on a salary plus commission. If they work on commission alone, they are paid a certain **commission rate,** or percent of their sales.

EXAMPLE Kim sells houses for a real estate company. She earns $3\frac{1}{2}\%$ of the selling price of the property. If Kim sells a house for $85,000, how much is her commission? Multiply $85,000 by $3\frac{1}{2}\%$ or 3.5% or 0.035.

Commission rate		Selling price		Amount of commission
0.035	×	$85,000	=	$2975

Write each commission rate as a decimal. Then multiply to find the amount of commission.

	Amount of Sales	Commission Rate	Decimal	Amount of Commission
1.	$125,000	3%		
2.	$96,400	2%		
3.	$100,000	2.5%		
4.	$68,900	3.5%		
5.	$174,100	$1\frac{1}{2}\%$		
6.	$32,491	5%		

7. Serene sells 1-year magazine subscriptions. She earns a commission of 25% of her sales. One evening, she sold $236 worth of subscriptions. How much commission did she earn?

Answer _____

8. Clyde Edison sells encyclopedias. He earns a commission of 15% for each sale. How much does he earn if the amount of the sale is $799.50?

Answer _____

9. Lena Chiu sells cosmetics and receives commissions of 45%. She sold $95 worth of cosmetics to one customer. How much commission did she earn?

Answer _____

10. Bill Barnes sells cleaning products on commission. He earns 40% commission on his sales. If he has sales of $983, how much commission does he earn?

Answer _____

EARNING MONEY

Salary plus Commission

Some salespersons earn both commission and a salary or hourly wage. The commission may be on all sales, or just sales above a certain amount.

EXAMPLE   In a men's clothing store, Pete is paid $248 per week and $10\frac{1}{2}\%$ on all sales over $2500. One week he sold a total of $3760. How much did he earn in salary plus commission that week?

> Sales for which commission is paid: $3760 − $2500 = $1260
> Commission: 0.105 × $1260 = $132.30
> Salary plus commission: $248 + $132.30 = $380.30

Solve.

1. Rita sells cars. She earns a salary of $800 per month, plus a commission of 2% on all sales. In December, Rita sold $149,000 worth of cars. What were her total earnings in December?

Answer _____

2. Elmer works in a computer store. He is paid a weekly salary of $180 and a commission of 4.5% of all sales. One week, he sold $9770 worth of merchandise. How much did Elmer earn that week?

Answer _____

3. Laura Lucas works in a furniture store. She earns $160 a week plus 6% of all sales over $2000. One week in January, Laura's total sales were $9400. What were Laura's earnings for that week?

Answer _____

4. Ted sells textbooks to schools. His company pays him a monthly salary of $980, plus a commission of $2\frac{1}{2}\%$ on the amount of sales. One busy month, Ted sold $213,000 worth of books. How much did he earn that month?

Answer _____

5. Carey has two job offers for sales jobs. For job A, he would earn a monthly salary of $2500 and no commission. For job B, he would earn $1000 per month and commission of 5% on all sales. Which would pay more if his sales are $50,000 per month?

Answer _____

6. Roberta works in a home appliance store. She is paid $195 per week and 3% on all sales over $1000. During one year, her average weekly sales were $7800. About how much did she earn each week? About how much did she earn during the year?

Answer _____

Making Bar Graphs

Bar graphs are useful for comparing quantities. The table below shows last month's sales by representatives of Superior Office Equipment.

Name of Representative	October Sales
Andy Avalos	$15,300
Bonnie Banes	$31,800
Carl Casper	$35,200
Donna Dixon	$19,000
Edward Evans	$26,500
Faye Farmer	$24,100

To make a bar graph from the information in the table, draw a bar beside each person's name to indicate the amount of sales. The bar beside *A. Avalos* is shown. Notice that it extends past the mark for 14 (thousands) on the horizontal scale. It is closer to 16 than to 14.

OCTOBER SALES BY SALES REPRESENTATIVE (IN THOUSANDS)

A. Avalos
B. Banes
C. Casper
D. Dixon
E. Evans
F. Farmer

0 2 4 6 8 10 12 14 16 18 20 22 24 26 28 30 32 34 36 38
Sales (1000s)

1. Complete the bar graph.

Answers

2. Each sales representative earns 15% commission on the total amount of sales. Which representative earned the most commission in October?

_____

3. How much commission was earned by the sales representative who sold the most?

_____

4. Which sales representative earned the least commission in October?

_____

5. How much commission was earned by the sales representative who sold the least?

_____

6. How many sales representatives had commissions of more than $3,000 in October?

_____

Employee Medical Insurance

Many employers offer group medical insurance to employees. This is an important benefit, since medical insurance provides financial protection in the event of a serious illness or injury. The company buys a group insurance policy and pays **premiums** for each employee to the insurance company. The insurance company then agrees to pay certain medical costs of the employees. Part or all of the cost of premiums may be deducted from an employee's pay.

The premiums for medical insurance depend on the specific costs that the insurance company will pay, the number of individuals covered by the insurance, and other factors. The table at the right shows premiums for two different medical insurance plans from *First Medical Insurance*.

—FIRST MEDICAL INSURANCE— Monthly Premiums		
	Plan A	Plan B
Single coverage	$125	$160
Family coverage	$205	$238

EXAMPLE Lila Shepard's employer pays 80% of the cost of group insurance through First Medical. Lila has Plan B, single coverage. How much is the employer's contribution each month for Lila's coverage? How much does Lila contribute each month?

Premium		Employer's percent		Employer's contribution
$160	×	0.80	=	$128

The employer pays $128. So, Lila pays $160 − $128 or $32.

Use the information above to complete the table.

(Hint: To find the annual contribution, multiply by 12.)

	Employee's Name	Plan	Monthly Premium	Employer's Percent	Employer's Contribution		Employee's Contribution	
					Monthly	Yearly	Monthly	Yearly
1.	Molly Rand	Family Plan A		50%				
2.	Brad Voltman	Single Plan A		90%				
3.	Chris West	Single Plan B		75%				
4.	Blake Horton	Family Plan B		20%				

5. Trish has two job offers. Company A offered her a salary of $19,000 and paid medical coverage worth $150 per month. Company B offered a salary of $1700 per month with no paid medical coverage. Which offer seems to be better?

6. Brent Goldman's employer pays 60% of the monthly medical premium of $234.00. The rest of the premium is deducted in equal portions from Brent's pay. If he is paid twice per month, how much is deducted each time?

Answer _____

Answer _____

Payroll Deductions

The amount an employee earns during a pay period is called the **gross pay.** However, the employer is required by the government to hold back certain amounts for federal taxes, state taxes, and social security (FICA). In addition, most employers hold back certain amounts for insurance. The employer pays these amounts to the government agencies and insurance companies on behalf of the employee.

The employee's paycheck is reduced by the amounts withheld. These payments for taxes and insurance are called **deductions.** The amount remaining after deductions are subtracted from earnings is the **net pay,** or take-home pay.

An employee's paycheck stub is shown below. What amount should be in the box for NET PAY?

EMPLOYEE NUMBER	PERIOD ENDING	HOURS	
		REGULAR	OVERTIME
108638	6/18/90	40	0

EARNINGS		
REGULAR	OVERTIME	GROSS PAY
364.40	0	364.40

DEDUCTIONS				NET PAY
FED. TAX	FICA	STATE TAX	MEDICAL INSURANCE	
41.86	27.37	10.93	15.50	

Total deductions: $41.86 + $27.37 + $10.93 + $15.50 = $95.66

Gross pay		Deductions		Net pay
$364.40	−	$95.66	=	$268.74

Complete each row of the chart to find the employee's net pay.

	Gross Pay	Deductions				Total Ded.	Net Pay
		Fed. Tax	State Tax	FICA	Med. Ins.		
1.	$550.00	$82.50	$22.00	$41.30	$7.50		
2.	$350.00	$32.00	$10.50	$26.29	$7.25		
3.	$350.00	$24.19	$9.80	$26.29	$42.70		
4.	$209.20	$16.74	$4.20	$15.71	0		
5.	$779.53	$155.90	$28.89	$58.54	$25.61		
6.	$658.44	$98.72	$19.76	$49.49	0		

7. In one pay period, Karen had $318.80 in regular earnings and $95.64 in overtime earnings. Her employer withheld $135.90 for taxes and insurance. What was Karen's take-home pay for that pay period?

Answer _____

Calculator Applications

When you multiply or divide with a calculator, the display may show several digits to the right of the decimal point. If the display is an amount of money, you will usually need to round to the nearest cent, dime, or dollar. Think about how accurate the answer needs to be.

EXAMPLE Molly is having dinner in a restaurant. She wants to leave a tip of about 15% of the bill. If the dinner costs $12.19, how much tip should she leave?

12.19 $\boxed{\times}$ .15 $\boxed{=}$ $\boxed{1.8285}$

Molly has several choices of how to round the number in the calculator display. For each choice shown below, one digit is underlined. Recall that to round the display, you should increase the underlined digit by 1 if the digit to the right is 5 or greater. Digits to the right should be dropped or changed to zero.

Nearest cent	Nearest dime	Nearest dollar
1.8285	1.8285	1.8285
$1.83	**$1.80**	**$2**

Molly decides to leave a tip of $1.80.

Look at each calculator display. Round to the nearest cent, dime, and dollar.

		Nearest cent	Nearest dime	Nearest dollar
1.	1.0935	$1.09	$1.10	$1
2.	14.2575			
3.	4.8915			
4.	0.807			
5.	2.6805			
6.	3.668			
7.	0.3975			
8.	15.558			

9. Joe and three of his friends had dinner at a restaurant. If the bill was $55.48, how much was the 15% tip? Round to the nearest dime.

10. Suppose Joe and his three friends evenly split the total cost of the dinner and tip. How much did each person contribute? Round to the nearest dollar.

Answer _____

Answer _____

Identify Substeps

Solving a problem requires several steps such as reading the problem, deciding what to do, and finding the answer. Some steps of solving the problem may need to be broken down into *substeps*, or smaller steps. Identifying the substeps is important in planning how to solve the main problem.

Read the problem.

In one week Wendy worked 42.5 hours. She earned overtime for each hour over 40. Her overtime rate was 1.5 times her regular rate of $8.70 per hour. What was her gross pay for the week?

Identify substeps.

1. How many hours of overtime pay did Wendy earn?
2. How much was she paid for each hour of overtime?
3. How much was the total overtime pay?
4. How much was the total pay for the 40 regular hours?

Solve the problem.

First find the answer for each substep.

1. $42.5 - 40 = 2.5$ hours overtime
2. $1.5 \times \$8.70 = \$13.05$ per hour of overtime
3. $2.5 \times \$13.05 = \$32.625$ or 32.63 total overtime pay
4. $40 \times \$8.70 = \$348.00$ total regular pay

Then solve the main problem.

Regular pay		Overtime pay		Gross pay
$348.00	+	$32.63	=	$380.63

Wendy's gross pay for the week was $380.63.

Write two substeps for each problem. Do not solve.

---

1. Georgette's gross pay for a week was $304.00. The deduction for state tax was 3% of her gross pay. Her other deductions totalled $56.24. What was Georgette's take-home pay for the week?

2. One week Billy worked 36 hours at $6.70 per hour. The next week he worked 40 hours at $6.85 per hour. How much more did he earn the second week?

Substep 1 _____

_____

Substep 2 _____

_____

Substep 1 _____

_____

Substep 2 _____

_____

Solve.

3. Solve each substep of Problem 1. Then solve the main problem.

Answer to Substep 1 _____

Answer to Substep 2 _____

Answer to main problem _____

4. Solve each substep of Problem 2. Then solve the main problem.

Answer to Substep 1 _____

Answer to Substep 2 _____

Answer to main problem _____

5. When Randy started his job, he earned $5.40 an hour. Now he makes $234 for working a 40-hour week. How much more does Randy earn per hour than he did when he started?

Answer _____

6. Evelyn earns a weekly salary of $560. Wanda earns a monthly salary of $2370. Who earns more per year? How much more?

Answer _____

7. Bonnie got a raise of 32¢ per hour. Now she earns $314.40 for a 40 hour week. What was her hourly rate before her raise?

Answer _____

8. Xavier earns a yearly salary of $16,500. If he gets a raise of $110 per month, what is the percent of increase?

Answer _____

9. One week, Christine earned 8% commission on sales of $4700. The next week, she earned 9% commission on sales of $5500. How much more commission did she earn the second week than the first week?

Answer _____

10. In one week, Quenton earned $72.90 for overtime hours. He earns time-and-a-half for overtime. If his regular rate is $8.10 per hour, how many hours of overtime did Quenton work?

Answer _____

EARNING MONEY

Retail Store Profits

Another very common way of earning money is to operate a retail store. In order to make money, the store operator must set prices high enough to pay the cost of the merchandise and the expenses of operating the store. The **gross income** is the total amount of money taken in from sales of merchandise. After cost of merchandise and other expenses are subtracted, the amount left is the **profit.**

EXAMPLE   Last year, the Green Front Grocery sold $250,000 worth of groceries. Cost of the groceries was $190,000. Rent, wages, utilities, and other expenses amounted to $40,000. What was the profit?

$$\underset{\$250,000}{\text{Gross income}} - \underset{(\$190,000 + \$40,000)}{\text{Expenses}} = \underset{\$20,000}{\text{Profit}}$$

What percent of gross income was the profit?

$$\underset{\$20,000}{\text{Profit}} \div \underset{\$250,000}{\text{Gross income}} = \underset{0.08 \text{ or } 8\%}{\text{Percent}}$$

Solve.

1. The Ideal Furniture Store did a total business of $156,000 during one month. The merchandise costs were $97,000. Other expenses amounted to $26,000. What was the profit?

Answer _____

2. A shoe merchant did a total business of $39,500. Cost of merchandise was $19,300, and expenses were $11,800. What was the profit?

Answer _____

3. The Breceda Meat Market did a total business of $52,000 in March. Cost of the meat was $35,000. Expenses amounted to $12,000. How much profit was made?

Answer _____

4. In March, what percent of Breceda Meat Market's gross income was profit?

Answer _____

5. Classic Clothing had total sales of $57,000 for April. Merchandise costs were $34,000. Other expenses were $11,000. What was the profit?

Answer _____

6. In April, what percent of Classic Clothing's gross income was profit?

Answer _____

EARNING MONEY

Markup, Overhead, and Profit

The difference between the cost and selling price is called **markup**. Expenses incurred in selling, such as rent, heating, lighting, wages, etc., are called **overhead**. Thus, markup must include both overhead and profit, as shown in this diagram.

After years of experience, a store owner or manager can estimate how much the overhead will be and how much markup to allow between the cost and the selling price. Sometimes the markup is expressed as a percent of the cost of an item.

EXAMPLE   Suppose a store owner pays $250 for a table, and allows a markup of 50% of the cost. For what price should the table be sold?

Markup = 50% of $250 = $125
Selling Cost = $250 + $125 = $375

The table should be sold for $375.

Solve.

1. A store manager paid $40 each for coats. The markup is 60%. For what price should the coats be sold?

Answer _____

2. A store owner bought belts at $96 per dozen. If the markup is 45%, what price should be marked on each belt? (Hint: First find the cost for each belt.)

Answer _____

3. Fresh foods must have a larger markup, since they are perishable. A grocer bought bananas for 32¢ per pound. If the markup is 100%, how much should the bananas be sold for?

Answer _____

4. A music store bought a trumpet for $400 and used a markup of 50% to set the selling price. A customer bought the trumpet on sale for 50% off. How much did the customer pay?

Answer _____

5. A store owner paid $35 each for sweaters. They were sold for $55. The overhead was $10. What was the profit on each sweater?

Answer _____

6. A men's store bought summer suits at $120, to be sold at $180. The suits left at the end of the summer were put on sale for $150. If the overhead was $40 per suit, what was the loss on each suit that was sold for $150?

Answer _____

Making a Line Graph

The table shows last year's monthly sales and overhead at Capitol Clothing. Sales are given in thousands of dollars. That is, 12 means $12,000 dollars. This data can be shown on a line graph. Trends and changes can be easily detected from the graph.

	Winter			Spring			Summer			Fall		
	Jan	Feb	Mar	Apr	May	June	July	Aug	Sept	Oct	Nov	Dec
Sales ($1000)	62	38	57	90	76	68	74	95	92	85	98	124
Overhead	29	24	24	22	20	20	28	30	25	27	30	35

This line graph has two lines, a solid line for sales and a dashed line for overhead. To finish the line showing the sales amounts, first make a dot for each month across from the correct place on the vertical scale. Then connect the dots with a solid line.

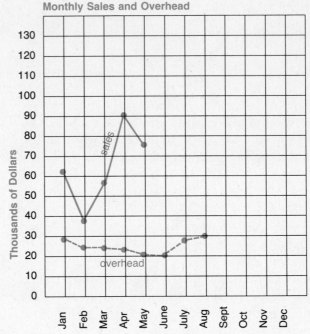

1. Complete the line showing sales each month. Connect the dots with a *solid* line.

2. Complete the line showing overhead each month. Connect the dots with a *dashed* line.

3. Which month had the most sales? _____

4. Which month had the least sales? _____

5. Which month had the most overhead? _____

6. Which months had the least overhead? _____

7. Was more money spent on overhead during winter or spring? _____

8. Were there more sales during the summer months or during the fall months? _____

9. Between what two months did sales go up the most? _____

10. Between what two months did sales go down the most? _____

EARNING MONEY

Self-Employment

Some people prefer to work for themselves rather than be an employee of another person or company. Here are some examples of people who are **self-employed.**

- Bob Cook has a mail-order business selling computer programs.
- Peter Seltzer does art work from his home.
- Dawn Fowler does childcare in her home.
- Toni Adams does lawncare for people in her neighborhood.
- Richard Riley sells reference books and earns commission from a company, but he plans his own work schedule and has an office in his own home.
- Mary Bennis gives music lessons from her home.

Self-employed persons are required to keep careful records and pay taxes on their profits. To determine the profits from self-employment, the expenses of doing business are deducted from earnings. Examples of expenses are costs for inventory (merchandise to sell), office equipment, phone service, mailing costs, supplies, and transportation. If a person operates a home-based business, a portion of the rent or mortgage may be counted as a business expense if certain conditions are met.

The chart shows last-year's self-employment expenses for the six people above. Find the total expenses for each person.

	Name	Inventory	Rent & Utilities	Equipment	Mail	Transportation	TOTAL EXPENSES
1.	B. Cook	$4780	$2422	$314	$549	$2409	$10,474
2.	P. Seltzer	0	1248	235	10	450	
3.	D. Fowler	0	3800	270	12	0	
4.	T. Adams	295	678	2504	58	4917	
5.	R. Riley	0	411	78	59	395	
6.	M. Bennis	0	0	15	10	35	

Suppose Bob Cook earned $20,400 during the year. To find his profit, subtract the expenses (from Exercise 1). His profit from self-employment was $20,400 − $10,474 or $9926.

For Exercises 7–11, copy each person's total expenses from the chart. Then subtract to find the profit.

	7. P. Seltzer	**8.** D. Fowler	**9.** T. Adams	**10.** R. Riley	**11.** M. Bennis
Earnings	$9700	$8450	$32,439	$4355	$2750
Expenses	−_____	−_____	−_____	−_____	−_____
Profit	_____	_____	_____	_____	_____

65

Profit Sharing

The Hi-Five Sports Equipment Company pays out 15% of its yearly profits as bonuses to employees with 5 or more years of service. These bonuses are distributed to employees through a **profit sharing** plan.

EXAMPLE   Last year Hi-Five's profits were $1,642,000. How much profit was distributed to the employees?

$$\$1,642,000 \times 0.15 = \$246,300$$

The profit sharing plan is based on a point system, according to the number of years of service: 1 point for 5-9 years, 2 points for 10-14 years, and 3 points for 15 or more years. To find the amount of the bonus for each point, $246,300 was divided by the total number of points.

Complete the chart to find the total number of points.

	Years of Service	Number of Employees	Points Each	Multiply Number of Employees by Points Each
1.	5-9	41		
2.	10-14	25		
3.	15+	18		
			4.	TOTAL POINTS:

5. Divide $246,300 by the answer to Exercise 4 to find out how much each point is worth. Round to the nearest dollar.

Answer _____

6. Find the amount of bonus for an employee with 12 years of service. (Hint: The employee is awarded two points.)

Answer _____

7. Find the amount of bonus for an employee with 20 years of service.

Answer _____

8. Last year the ABX Company paid out 12% of its $3,377,000 profits in bonuses. Each of its 80 employees got an equal share. How much did each employee get?

Answer _____

9. The Janyln Company uses a point system for the profit-sharing plan. Of the 45 employees eligible for the plan in 1990, 13 received two points each and the rest received 1 point each. What was the total number of points?

Answer _____

10. The Janlyn Company paid out 10.5% of its profits in 1990. Their profits were $827,400. To the nearest cent, how much was each point worth? Use the total number of points from Exercise 9.

Answer _____

Business Travel Expenses

Mildred Jackson often travels on company business. She keeps a record of the money she spends and saves the receipts. She must also write down information such as the business purpose for the expenses and the locations where she stayed. When she returns, she turns in her records and is reimbursed, or paid back, by the company for the business expenses. The company must keep the records and receipts for tax purposes.

EXAMPLE On one business trip, Mildred stayed 3 nights at a hotel where the room rate was $65.50 per night, plus 8.9% hotel tax. To find the cost of her room for 3 nights, multiply. Then find the amount of tax and add.

Number of nights   Rate per night
         3   × $65.50   = $196.50

Hotel tax: 0.089 × $196.50 = $17.49
Total cost including tax: $196.50 + $17.49 = $213.99

Solve.

1. On another business trip, Mildred Jackson spent 4 nights at a motel that cost $30.75 per night plus 11% hotel tax. What were her room expenses on this trip?

2. Mildred Jackson's total cost, including tax, for hotel rooms on a 6-day trip was $459. What was the average cost per night?

Answer _____

Answer _____

After business trips, Mildred Jackson is also paid back for her meals and transportation expenses. The tables at the right show meal and transportation expenses on a 3-day trip.

Complete the tables by finding the total of each row and each column. When you have finished, the right column and bottom row should have the same sum. Write this amount in the lower right corner.

	MEALS			
Date	Breakfast	Lunch	Dinner	Totals
3. May 15	$3.75	$4.50	$8.50	
4. May 16	$2.85	$5.00	$10.50	
5. May 17	$3.50	$3.95	$9.50	
6. Totals				

	TRANSPORTATION		
Date	Air Fares	Rental Cars & Gasoline	Totals
7. May 15	$315	$30	
8. May 16		$30	
9. May 17	$275	¢30 + $5 gas	
10. Totals			

Disability Pay

Many companies provide **disability insurance** for their employees. If an employee becomes ill or injured and cannot work for an extended period of time, the insurance company pays part of the employee's salary. The illness or injury does not have to be job-related; it can be a result of a car accident or a medical problem.

Usually, the insurance company pays 50-80% of the disabled employee's salary each week for a defined period of time, such as 6 months. This **disability pay** ends after the defined period, or sooner if the employee is able to return to work.

EXAMPLE   Shaun had surgery for a back injury and was unable to work for 30 weeks. His company's disability insurance pays 50% of an employee's weekly salary for up to 26 weeks. Shaun's weekly salary was $450. How much disability pay did he receive each week? What was the total amount of disability pay that he received?

Disability pay each week: $50\% \times \$450 = 0.5 \times \$450 = \$225$
Total disability pay (26 weeks): $26 \times \$225 = \$5850$

For each problem, find the employee's disability pay per week and the total disability pay.

	Disability pay per week	Total disability pay
1. Aretha is disabled for 25 weeks. Her weekly salary is $380. The disability insurance pays 50% of her salary for up to 1 year.		
2. Corky is disabled for 36 weeks. His weekly salary is $360. The disability insurance pays 75% of his salary for up to 1 year.		
3. George's disability insurance pays 80% of his salary for up to 18 months. He earns $950 per week, and is disabled for 42 weeks.		
4. Kwan's disability insurance pays 50% of his salary for up to 2 years. His weekly salary is $578, and he is disabled for 81 weeks.		
5. Paulette's disability insurance pays 60% of her salary for up to 24 months. Her weekly salary is $785. She is disabled for 65 weeks.		
6. Donna has disability insurance that pays 80% of her weekly salary for up to 4 years. Her weekly salary is $1230. She is disabled for more than 5 years.		

EARNING MONEY

Retirement Income

Two sources of income for retired people are **social security** and **pensions**. More than 90% of American workers have a payroll deduction for social security tax. These workers and their spouses will receive monthly social security payments when they retire at age 62 or older. Social security payments alone are not usually enough to cover living expenses of a retired worker.

An employee who retires after working many years for the same company may get a pension from the company. The amount of a pension payment is based on the person's salary while employed, the age at retirement, and other factors.

In addition to social security and pensions, certain types of savings accounts and investments are designed to provide retirement income. By planning and saving money *before* retirement, a worker can make sure that retirement income will cover living expenses.

EXAMPLE Find the monthly income from a retirement account that provides annual income of $1860.

Yearly income		Months per yr		Monthly income
$1860	÷	12	=	$155

Solve.

1. Velma Parks gets $460 per month from social security, and has no other income. What is her yearly income?

Answer _____

2. Sol Brandau gets a monthly pension of $984 and a monthly social security check of $475. What is his yearly income from these two sources?

Answer _____

3. During last year, Jack Dooley received $3,290 from a retirement account. He also got $621 per month from social security. What was his average monthly income from these two sources?

Answer _____

4. Before she retired, Victoria Hall's yearly salary was $18,200. Now she gets $605 per month from a pension plan and $525 from social security. How much less is she earning per year now?

Answer _____

5. Brad Benson is 62 years old. If he waits until age 65 to retire, he will get $717 per month in social security payments. If he retires now, he will get 80% of that amount. How much will the payments be if Brad Benson retires now?

Answer _____

6. Each month Marsha Mason gets $773 from her company pension and $532 from social security. Her living expenses are about $1550 per month. About how much money from savings will she need each month?

Answer _____

PROBLEM-SOLVING STRATEGY

Use a Bar Graph

The graph shows the average weekly earnings of people in manufacturing industries. The information in the graph can be used to solve problems.

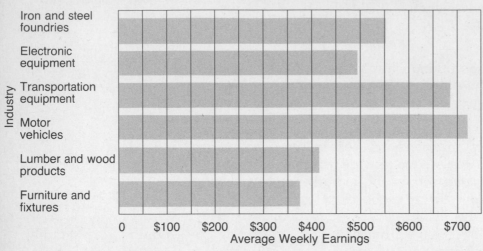

AVERAGE WEEKLY EARNINGS IN MANUFACTURING INDUSTRIES

Read the problem.

Workers in the electronic equipment industry work about 41 hours per week. What is their average hourly wage?

Read the graph for data.

Look at the bar labeled electronic equipment and read the scale. If the end of the bar is between two numbers on the scale, estimate the length. Then write down the data.

Average weekly earnings: $490

Solve the problem.

Divide the weekly wage by the hours per week.

$490 ÷ 41 = $11.95

Solve. Use the bar graph above.

---

1. On the average, how much more is earned per week by workers in the transportation equipment industry than by workers in the lumber and wood products industry?

   Answer _____

2. Workers in the furniture and fixtures industry work about 39 hours per week. What is their average hourly wage?

   Answer _____

---

3. What is the average yearly salary for workers in iron and steel foundries?

   Answer _____

4. What is the average yearly salary for workers in the motor vehicle industry?

   Answer _____

PROBLEM-SOLVING STRATEGY
Use a Line Graph

A line graph may be used to show how data can change over a period of time. A double-line graph, such as the one below, is helpful for comparing sets of data.

Pat and Chris are hired by the same company. Each person will earn $10,000 the first year. Pat gets an increase of $2,000 each year. Chris gets an increase of 20% each year. The line graph at the right shows changes in their salaries over 5 years.

Read the problem.
> In Year 4, about how much higher is Chris's salary than Pat's salary?

Read the graph for data.
> Look above Year 4 on the horizontal scale. Find the point for Chris's salary. Trace an imaginary line from the point to the scale on the left. If the value is between two numbers on the scale, estimate. Write down the data for Chris's salary. Use the same method to find Pat's salary

> Chris's salary: about $17,300

> Pat's salary: $16,000

Solve the problem.
> $17,300 − $16,000 = $1,300

> In Year 4, Chris earns about $1,300 more than Pat.

YEARLY SALARIES

Solve. Use the line graph above.

1. In Year 5, about how much higher is Chris's salary than Pat's salary?

    Answer _____

2. What is the percent of increase in Pat's salary from Year 3 to Year 4?

    Answer _____

3. What is the percent of increase in Pat's salary from Year 4 to Year 5?

    Answer _____

4. In Year 4, about how much is Chris's salary per week?

    Answer _____

5. In Year 5, about how much is Pat's salary per week?

    Answer _____

6. Predict the difference between Chris's salary and Pat's salary in Year 6.

    Answer _____

EARNING MONEY

Making Circle Graphs

A circle graph can help you compare parts of a whole, or quantities that total 100%. For example, a person's yearly income is a whole amount that can be represented by a circle. The circle can be divided into parts to represent way the income was earned. You would *not* make a circle graph from a list of incomes of several *different* people, because the people do not represent a whole.

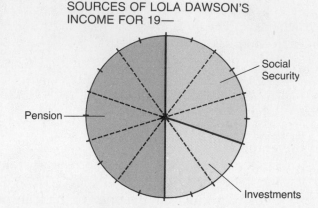

SOURCES OF LOLA DAWSON'S INCOME FOR 19—

Social Security

Pension

Investments

If a circle is divided into 10 parts, each part is 10% of the whole. The circle graph at the right shows sources of Lola Dawson's income. The graph shows that 3 tenths or 30% was social security.

1. What percent of Lola's income

   was from her pension? _____

2. What percent of Lola's income

   was from investments? _____

To make a circle graph when you know the total amount and several parts, first find the percent of the total that each part represents.

EXAMPLE   Randy Eisen's income from several sources for one year was $15,900. Of the total, $6960 was from social security. What percent of the total was from social security?

Randy Eisen's Income 19—	
Social security	$ 6960
Pension	4134
Interest	1610
Part-time job	3196
TOTAL	$15,900

Social security	Total income	Decimal to nearest hundredth
$6960	÷ $15,900 =	0.438 or 0.44

Write the decimal as a percent. 0.44 = 44%

Find the percent of Randy's income from each source. Use the table.

3. Pension _____   4. Interest _____   5. Part-time job _____

6. Complete the circle graph of Randy Eisen's Income.

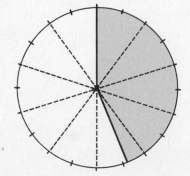

7. Did social security contribute more or less than half of Randy Eisen's income? _____

8. Which source contributed about one-fourth of Randy Eisen's income? _____

9. Which source contributed about one-fifth of the income? _____

EARNING MONEY
Unit 3 Review

Solve.

1. Liz earns $832 for a 40-hour work week. She earns $12.48 for each hour of overtime. How much does she earn for a 44-hour week?

   Answer _____

2. Eric is a computer programmer that earns a yearly salary of $35,400. What is his weekly salary?

   Answer _____

3. Norma sells sports equipment. She earns a salary of $240 per work plus commission of 3% on all sales. One week she had sales of $3500. How much did she earn that week?

   Answer _____

4. In one pay period, Jack had $562.30 in regular earnings. His employer withheld $124.30 for taxes and $47.15 for insurance. What was Jack's take-home pay for that pay period?

   Answer _____

5. Henry's disability insurance pays 70% of his salary for up to 26 weeks. If his weekly salary is $450 and he is disabled for 20 weeks, how much disability pay will he get?

   Answer _____

6. Carrie has a monthly retirement income of $400 from a pension, $465 from social security, $375 from investments, and $200 from a part-time job. What is her total monthly retirement income?

   Answer _____

7. Complete the line graph for the table.

Tessoni's Windows Spring & Summer Sales
(Thousands of dollars)

April	45
May	70
June	75
July	55
Aug	50
Sept	30

8. Ralph works part-time and has a yearly income of $5600, including a salary of $3750, and tips of $1850. What percent of his income was from his salary? What percent of his income was from his tips?

   Answer _____

   Make a circle graph to show his income.

9. Look at the graph in Exercise 7. Between what 2 months did the sales increase the most?

   Answer _____

10. A store owner bought hats for $6.50 each and sold them for $12. The overhead was $2.50. What was the profit on each hat?

   Answer _____

Comparing Prices

"A penny saved is a penny earned." A wise shopper can save money by comparing prices at different stores and by buying at discount prices. A **discount** is an amount subtracted from the regular price, often a percent of the regular price.

Some items are not priced individually. When comparing prices you may need to find the **unit price,** or the cost for one. If the cost does not divide evenly, round up to the next cent.

EXAMPLE Store A has scarves that are normally $4 each on sale at a 20% discount. Store B has the same type of scarves at 3 for $10. What is the price for a scarf at each store? Which store's price for a scarf is less?

STORE A
Discount: 20% of $4
$\qquad$ $0.2 \times \$4 = \$0.80$
Sale price: $\$4.00 - 0.80 = \$3.20$

STORE B
Find the unit price by dividing $10 by 3.
$$\frac{\$3.333}{3)\$10.00} = \$3.34$$

Since $3.20 is less than $3.34, Store A's price is less.

Find the amount of discount and the discount price of each item at Store A.

	Item	Reg. Price	Rate of Discount	Amount of Discount	Discount Price
1.	Camera	$32.50	10%	*$3.25*	
2.	Shoes	$39.50	15%		
3.	Bath towel	$6.00	25%		
4.	Shirt	$14.00	20%		
5.	File box	$8.80	50%		
6.	Radio	$12.49	$33\frac{1}{3}\%$		

7. The price of bath towels at Store B is 3 for $12. How much is the unit price? Is the price more or less than the sale price from Exercise 3?

Answer _____

8. The price of file boxes at Store B is 5 for $19.00. How much is the unit price? Is the price more or less than the sale price from Exercise 5?

Answer _____

9. The price of shirts at Store B is 2 for $25. How much is the unit price? Is the price more or less than the sale price from Exercise 4?

Answer _____

10. The regular price of shoes is $45. If the shoes are on sale at a discount of 30%, what is the sale price? Is the price more or less than the sale price from Exercise 2?

Answer _____

HANDLING MONEY
Using a Cash Account

A **cash account** is an itemized statement of income and expenses. To start a cash account, first label the columns on a ledger book or spreadsheet. Include columns for date, description, receipts, and different types of expenses such as food, clothing, housing, transportation, savings & giving. Label one column OTHER or MISC for miscellaneous expenses such as recreation. Write the current balance in the last column.

To use the cash account, list the date and description of each receipt or expense during the month and list the amount in the appropriate column. Add or subtract to find the balance. At the end of each month, find the total of each column. Then start a new page for the next month.

Study the cash account shown below. Then write each of these amounts in the cash account, finding the new balance each time.

1. 1/8   Shoes $43.78
2. 1/10   Gasoline $14.50
3. 1/12   Utility bills $85.79
4. 1/15   Car payment $157.00
5. 1/16   Groceries $78.11
6. 1/19   Wages $398.00
7. 1/22   Contributions $40.00
8. 1/24   Game tickets $16.40
9. 1/27   Savings $50.00
10. 1/30 Rent $240.00

| Date | Description | Receipts | Expenses | | | | | Balance |
			Food & Clothes	Housing & Utilities	Transpor-tation	Savings & Giving	Misc	$240.90
1/2	Groceries		58.09					182.81
1/5	Wages	370.00						552.81
1/8	Contribution					37.00		515.81
1/8	Shoes		43.78					472.03
	TOTALS							

11. For the cash account above, find the total for the receipts and for each column of expenses.

12. Find the total of all the expenses. Is this amount more or less than the receipts?

Answer _____

HANDLING MONEY

Preparing a Monthly Budget

A **budget** is a plan of how and in what amount income is to be spent. Whether you are choosing an apartment or buying new clothes, having a budget helps you know how much you can afford to spend.

To prepare a budget, you should look at your current spending records and estimate the amount needed for each budget category. Make sure to include savings and giving, and to allow for occasional expenses such as car insurance and repairs. Add the amounts budgeted for each category and compare this to your income (take-home pay). If the expenses are more or less than the income, **balance** the budget by adjusting the amounts for certain categories.

---

1. The list at the right shows Natalie's expenses for an average month. Find the total.

Answer _____

2. Natalie's monthly income is $1070. Are the expenses less or more than the income?

Answer _____

NATALIE'S EXPENSES

Food & clothes	**$220**
Housing & utilities	**$430**
Transportation	**$90**
Savings & giving	**$100**
Miscellaneous	**$120**

---

3. Natalie can balance her budget by putting more money in savings. How much more per month can she save?

Answer _____

4. Natalie wants to buy a car. If she does, her transportation costs increase to $240 per month. Can she afford to buy a car without reducing other amounts in the budget?

Answer _____

---

5. Lavon's income is $1300 per month. Here is his monthly budget except for food and clothes. To balance the budget, how much can he spend for food and clothes?

Housing & utilities	$280
Transportation	$320
Savings & giving	$130
Miscellaneous	$170

Food & clothes $ _____

6. Edna Liebman is retired and has an income of $680 per month. Here is her monthly budget except for miscellaneous expenses. To balance the budget, how much can she spend for miscellaneous expenses?

Food & clothes	$160
Housing & utilities	$190
Transportation	$100
Savings & giving	$110

Miscellaneous $ _____

---

7. Chun Lee buys clothing during January and July when the prices are lowest. If he spends a total of $420, how much should he set aside each month for clothing?

Answer _____

8. The Alpert family takes a vacation each year that costs about $1600. What amount should be saved or set aside each month for vacation expenses?

Answer _____

HANDLING MONEY
Family Budgets

Circle graphs are helpful for showing the portion, or percent, that is budgeted for each category. The two circle graphs show monthly budgets for the Moore family and the Pasko family.

Pasko Family Budget (Income of $1730)

Moore Family Budget (Income of $2280)

Which family has a higher percent budgeted for food and clothes each month?

Since 39% is greater than 32%, the Pasko family's budget includes a greater percent for food and clothes. However, the *amount* budgeted on food depends on the income of each family.

Find the amount that each family has budgeted for each category.
(Hint: Write the percent as a decimal and multiply by the income.)

1. Pasko Family (Income of $1730 per month)

Food & clothes	$1730 \times 0.39 =$ _____
Housing & utilities	_____
Transportation	_____
Savings & giving	_____
Miscellaneous	_____
TOTAL	_____

2. Moore Family (Income of $2280 per month)

Food & clothes	$2280 \times 0.32 =$ _____
Housing & utilities	_____
Transportation	_____
Savings & giving	_____
Miscellaneous	_____
TOTAL	_____

3. Which family budgets a greater amount each month for food and clothes? Use your answers from Exercises 1 and 2.

Answer _____

4. Which family budgets a greater amount each month for transportation? Use your answers from Exercises 1 and 2.

Answer _____

5. Suppose each family saves 5% of its income each month. How much does each family save?

Answer _____

6. Suppose each family spends $100 a month for recreation. What percent does each family spend for recreation?

Answer _____

Checking Accounts

Many people write checks to pay for purchases or bills. Using a checking account is safer than paying cash, and both you and the bank will have records of how much is spent.

Opening a checking account at a bank requires a deposit and your signature on a signature card. The bank will give you some checks and deposit slips, then order printed checks that you will receive in about a week. Banks usually charge a monthly fee for checking accounts.

The amount of a check is written in both words and numbers. If there is a difference in these amounts, the bank will honor the amount written in words.

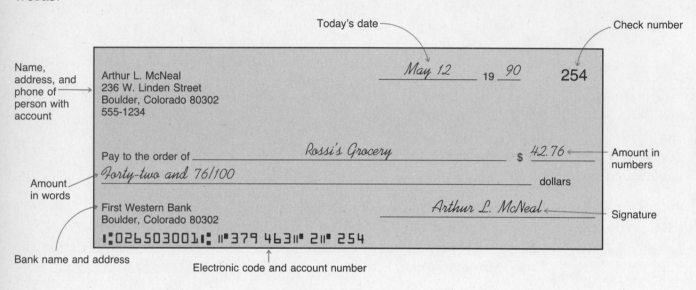

Write each amount in words as it would appear on a check.

1. $15.20 _____

2. $40.10 _____

3. $243.08 _____

4. $106.90 _____

5. Suppose you must pay $75.10 to Long's Hardware Store. Complete the check below for that amount using today's date and your name.

_____ 19___   **158**

Pay to the order of _____ $ _____

_____ dollars

First Western Bank
Boulder, Colorado 80302

_____

Check Registers

A **check register** is sent to you with your checks to keep track of the checks you write, deposits you make, and the balance you have left in your checking account. This register page shows two check payments and one deposit. After each entry, you add or subtract to find the current balance in the account.

Number	Date	Transaction	Payment/Debit		Deposit/Credit		Balance		
							724	59	← Read this as $724.59.
457	5/7	Weinstein's Nursery	38	82			− 38	82	
		(garden supplies)					685	77	← New Balance
458	5/10	Mrs. Phyllis Kortney	375	00			−375	00	
		(rent)					310	77	← New Balance
	5/15	Deposit			872	36	+872	36	
		(paycheck)					1183	13	← New Balance

1. Find the three new balances in the right column.

Number	Date	Transaction	Payment/Debit		Deposit/Credit		Balance	
							974	82
145	12/2	South City Edison	83	70			83	70
		(electric bill)						
146	12/8	World Cable	14	57			14	57
		(Cable TV)						
	12/9	Deposit			475	80	475	80
		(Paycheck)						

2. On July 13, Maria deposited her paycheck for $650.25. Enter this amount in the Deposit/Credit column. Then complete all entries in the Balance column.

Number	Date	Transaction	Payment/Debit		Deposit/Credit		Balance	
							1075	65
175	7/10	Alfred's Furniture	153	58			153	58
		(kitchen table)						
176	7/12	New Jersey Bell	34	79			34	79
		(telephone bill)						
	7/13	deposit						
		(paycheck)						

PROBLEM-SOLVING STRATEGY
Make a List

Sometimes it helps to make a list to solve a problem. When you put information in a list in an organized way, it is easy to see how to solve the problem.

Read the problem.

When you open a checking account, you get to choose a design for the checks and a color for the checkbook cover. Suppose you can choose a design with pictures of the seashore, animals, or hearts. The color for the cover can be red, blue, green, or tan. How many different combinations of check design and color are possible?

Make a list.

Label the designs S, A, and H. Label the colors R, B, G, and T. Then make a list of possibilities. Be sure the list is organized carefully.

Seashore	Animals	Hearts
S-R	A-R	H-R
S-B	A-B	H-B
S-G	A-G	H-G
S-T	A-T	H-T

Solve the problem.

Count the number of combinations listed. There are 12 different combinations of design and color.

Make a list. Use your list to solve the problem.

1. The checks in Dwayne's checkbook are numbered from 1051 to 1075. How many of the check numbers are odd numbers?

2. The Underwood family is planning a vacation. They are going to a museum, to an amusement park, and to a zoo. They are deciding the order in which to visit each place. How many different orders are possible?

Answer _____

Answer _____

Make a list. Use your list to solve the problem.

3. The checks in Ralph's checkbook are numbered from 530 to 550. How many of the checks in the book have two digits that are the same? (Hint: 550 has two fives.)

Answer _____

4. The checks in Rachel's checkbook are numbered from 777 to 800. How many of the check numbers have digits with a sum greater than 20? (Hint: The digits of 777 have a sum of $7 + 7 + 7 = 21$.)

Answer _____

5. A snack bar sells small glasses of juice for $0.75 and large glasses of juice for $0.95. Cold sandwiches cost $1.10 and hot sandwiches cost $1.30. If a person buys one sandwich and one glass of juice, how many different total costs are possible?

Answer _____

6. The Spencer family is going shopping. They need to stop at the bookstore, grocery, shoestore, and pharmacy. They are deciding the order in which to visit each place. The grocery must be the third or fourth stop. How many different orders are possible?

Answer _____

7. The balance in Andrea's checkbook was $450.55. When she copied the balance, she accidentally reversed two adjacent digits. How many different amounts could Andrea have written?

Answer _____

8. The balance in Tony's checkbook was an exact number of dollars between $110 and $180. The last digit of the number was 4. How many such amounts are possible?

Answer _____

Savings Accounts: Simple Interest

When a customer deposits money in a savings account, the bank pays the customer for the use of the money. This payment is called **interest.** The formula $I = p \times r \times t$ is used to find **simple interest,** or interest on a specific amount at a fixed rate. When using the formula, express the rate, r, as a decimal.

> $$I = p \times r \times t$$
> **I**   is the amount of interest.
> **p**   is the principal, or amount of money in the savings account.
> **r**   is the rate, or percent of interest per year.
> **t**   is the time, or number of years.

EXAMPLE   If the principal is $500 and the rate is 7%, how much interest would be earned in 3 months?

Since the rate is based on years, change 3 months to $\frac{1}{4}$ or 0.25 year.

Principal	Rate	Time	Interest
p	× r	× t	= I
$500	× 0.07	× 0.25	= $8.75

Complete each row of the chart.

	Principal	Rate	Time in Months	Time in Years	p × r × t = Interest
1.	$500	7%	12	*1*	*500 × .07 × 1 =*
2.	$1000	7%	6	$\frac{1}{2}$ or 0.5	
3.	$800	9%	4		
4.	$500	6%	3		
5.	$1200	5.5%	12		
6.	$900	5.2%	9		

7. Julie Barstow deposited $400 in a savings account at 5% interest. How much interest will she earn in 9 months?

Answer _____

8. Esther withdrew her savings at the end of $\frac{1}{2}$ year. If she had deposited $750 at 6%, how much interest did she get? What was the amount she withdrew?

Answer _____

9. Milton Russell has $300 in a savings account at 9% interest. How much interest will he earn in 3 months?

Answer _____

10. If $1000 is deposited at 6% interest, how much interest is earned each month? How long will it take to earn $40 interest?

Answer _____

HANDLING MONEY

Savings Accounts: Compound Interest

Patricia deposited $100 in a savings account at 5% interest. At the end of 1 year, she will have $5 in interest. If Patricia leaves the $5 in the account, her new principal will be $105. During the second year, the bank will pay interest on the original principal *plus* the interest that has been added to the account. Interest paid in this way is said to be compounded annually (once a year).

EXAMPLE How much interest will be in Patricia's account at the end of the second year?

Interest for first year:

p	×	r	×	t	=	I
$100	×	0.05	×	1	=	$5.00

Account balance at end of first year:

Prior balance		Interest		New balance
$100	+	$5	=	$105

Interest for second year:

$105 × 0.05 × 1 = $5.25

Account balance at end of second year:

| $105 | + | $5.25 | = | $110.25 |

At the end of the second year the balance is $110.25.

Solve.

1. George has $250 in the savings bank and gets 5% interest compounded annually. How much interest will he get for the second year?

   Answer _____

2. Madge has $300 in her savings account and is paid 6% interest compounded annually. How much will she have in her account at the end of the second year?

   Answer _____

3. Pat has $500 in a savings account which earns 10% interest. How much will he have in the bank at the end of the second year if the interest is compounded annually?

   Answer _____

4. Evita has $170 in a savings account. She is paid 6% interest compounded annually. How much will she have in her account at the end of the second year?

   Answer _____

5. Ruth Russell deposited $350 in a savings account. She received 6% interest compounded semiannually (twice per year). How much interest did the account earn during the second half of the year? (Hint: Use 0.5 for the time.)

   Answer _____

6. Frank has $500 in a savings account and is paid 5% interest compounded semiannually. How much will he have in the account at the beginning of the second year?

   Answer _____

Savings Accounts: Daily Compounding

Because computers can make complex computations quickly, many banks offer interest compounded daily rather than yearly. With yearly compounding, a deposit of $100 at 5% earns $5 in 365 days, or about 1.37 cents per day ($5 ÷ 365). If interest is compounded daily the account will earn more than $5 in a year. This is because interest is added to the account each day and the interest earns interest.

If the **stated rate** is 5% and interest is compounded daily, the **effective rate** for one year would be 5.13%. With daily compounding, a deposit of $100 would earn $5.13 interest in one year. The table shows effective interest rates for various stated rates.

Stated Rate	Effective Annual Rate (Daily Compounding)
5%	5.13%
6%	6.18%
7%	7.25%
8%	8.32%
9%	9.41%
10%	10.67%

EXAMPLE The stated rate of interest on a savings account is 6%. If interest is compounded daily, how much annual interest would be earned on a deposit of $400?

The effective annual rate is 6.18%.

Principal		Effective Annual Rate		Annual Interest
$400	×	0.0618	=	$24.72

Complete each row of the chart to find the annual interest. The interest is compounded daily.

	Principal	Stated Rate	Effective Annual Rate	Annual Interest
1.	$1000	7%	7.25% or 0.0725	$1000 × 0.0725 =
2.	$5000	8%		
3.	$850	5%		
4.	$1130	10%		
5.	$280	9%		
6.	$585	6%		

7. Suppose an account of $1000 earns simple interest at 7% for one year. How much interest is earned?

8. Compare the answers to Exercises 1 and 7. How much more interest is earned when interest is compounded daily?

Answer _____

Answer _____

HANDLING MONEY

Calculator Applications

The diagram below leads to a shortcut that is helpful when calculating compound interest.

Suppose you need to find the new balance after 5% interest is added. The prior balance is 100% of itself. The interest is 5% of the prior balance. So, the new balance is 100% + 5%, or 105% of the prior balance.

Prior balance 100%	Interest 5%
New balance 105%	

EXAMPLE   Suppose interest is compounded quarterly and the rate is 6% per year or 1.5% per quarter. An account has $470 at the beginning of a year. How much is in the account at the end of the year?

Note that 100% + 1.5% is 101.5%. So, to find the balance at the end of each quarter, multiply the prior balance by 101.5% or 1.015.

Quarter	Key Sequence	New Balance	
1st	470 ⊗ 1.015 = 477.05	$477.05	(Note: Do not clear the display.)
2nd	⊗ 1.015 = 484.20575	$484.21	
3rd	⊗ 1.015 = 491.46884	$491.47	
4th	⊗ 1.015 = 498.84087	$498.84	

The balance at the end of the year is $498.84.

Solve. Use a calculator.

1. Suppose the prior balance was $200. By what number would you multiply to find the new balance after 9% interest is added? What is the new balance?

Answer _____

2. Suppose the prior balance was $350. By what number would you multiply to find the new balance after 5.2% interest is added? What is the new balance?

Answer _____

3. A savings account earns 5% interest compounded quarterly. If the account has $600 at the beginning of the year, how much is in the account at the end of the year? (Hint: Since the quarterly interest rate is 1.25%, multiply by 1.0125 four times.)

Answer _____

4. Suppose $100 is deposited in a savings account that has an effective annual rate of 5.3%. How much money would be in the account in 5 years? (Hint: Multiply by 1.053 five times.)

Answer _____

U.S. Savings Bonds

Series EE Savings Bonds can be purchased with face values of $50, $75, $100, $200, $500, $1000, $2000, and $10,000. The cost of these bonds is one-half the face value. For example, the cost of a $500 bond is $250. Each bond **matures,** or reaches its face value, in 8 to 12 years.

The bond can be **redeemed,** or cashed in, any time after 6 months. The **redemption value** of the bond includes interest for the time the bond was owned. The actual interest rate may change every 6 months, but a minimum rate of about 6% is guaranteed. The guaranteed redemption values for a $50 Series EE Savings Bond are shown in the table.

Series EE $50 Savings Bonds	
Time	Redemption Value
1 yr	$26.08
2 yr	$27.40
3 yr	$29.00
4 yr	$31.06
5 yr	$33.60
6 yr	$35.66
7 yr	$37.82
8 yr	$40.12
9 yr	$42.58
10 yr	$45.16

EXAMPLE   What is the redemption value of a $1000 bond after 5 years?
The redemption value of any bond is based on the redemption value of a $50 bond.

Value of $50 bond after 5 years		Number of $50 bonds equal to $1000 bond (1000 ÷ 50)		Redemption value of $1000 bond after 5 years
$33.60	×	20	=	$672.00

Solve. Use the table of redemption values.

1. Alex buys four $200 savings bonds. How much does he pay for them?

Answer _____

2. Wanda buys five $75 savings bonds. How much does she pay for them?

Answer _____

3. Norm Pulaski buys a $100 savings bond. What will be the redemption value in 4 years?

Answer _____

4. Agnes Barclay buys ten $50 savings bonds. What will be their total worth in 5 years?

Answer _____

5. Marlene spent $2500 for bonds. What is the minimum that the bonds will be worth in 10 years?

Answer _____

6. If Marlene puts $2500 in savings at 5% interest compounded daily, she would have $4072 in 10 years. Which is a better investment, a savings account at 5% or Series EE bonds?

Answer _____

HANDLING MONEY

Certificates of Deposit

Most banks offer certificates of deposit as well as savings accounts. A **certificate of deposit,** or CD, earns a higher interest rate than a savings account. The table at the right shows the interest rates that one bank was offering during a certain week.

Notice that the certificates require a minimum deposit, and the money must be left in the account for a certain period of time. If the money is withdrawn early the customer is charged a penalty, often 3 months interest.

FIRST BANK		Week of July 20, 19--
Certificates of Deposit	Minimum Deposit	Yearly Interest Rate
3 months	$5000	7.9%
6 months	$2500	8.0%
9 months	$2000	8.0%
1 year	$1000	8.1%

A customer invested $2400 in a 9-month CD that has a yearly interest rate of 8.5%. How much interest will the customer receive at the end of 9 months?

$$\text{Principal} \quad \text{Rate (8.5\%)} \quad \text{Time } (\tfrac{9}{12}\text{ yr}) \quad \text{Interest}$$
$$\$2400 \quad \times \quad 0.085 \quad \times \quad 0.75 \quad = \$153.00$$

Complete each row of the chart.

	Principal	Rate	Time in Months	Time in Years	p × r × t = Interest
1.	$5000	6.5%	6	$\frac{1}{2}$ or 0.5	$5000 × 0.065 × 0.5 =
2.	$1500	7.0%	12		
3.	$3500	6.9%	9		
4.	$7200	7.6%	3		
5.	$2000	6.4%	12		
6.	$2500	8.0%	6		

7. John Ramirez invested $5000 in a 6-month CD that earns 8.5%. How much interest will he receive at the end of 6 months?

Answer _____

8. Willa Smith bought a 9-month CD with an interest rate of 6.9%. If she invests $2000, how much interest will she get at the end of 9 months?

Answer _____

9. Margaret has two $3000 CDs, each for 6 months at 8.1%. How much interest will she get from her CDs?

Answer _____

10. Alex puts $4000 in a 1-year CD at 8.1%. At the end of 6 months, he withdraws the money and is charged a penalty of 3 months interest. How much interest does he receive?

Answer _____

Stocks

Many people invest money by purchasing **stocks.** A person who owns a share of stock is a partial owner of the company or business that issues the stock. The company uses money from the sale of stocks to help run the company. If the company makes a profit during the year, owners of stock are given **dividends,** or portions of the profit.

Suppose a business issued 5000 shares of stock. Jan Karlin bought 1000 shares. If the business gives out $15,000 in dividends, how much will Jan receive in dividends on her shares?

Jan Karlin owns $\frac{1000}{5000}$ or 0.20 or 20% of the stock. She will get 20% of $15,000, or $3000 in dividends.

Solve.

1. Myron Nelson bought stock in a manufacturing company. The first year he was paid a dividend of $5.25 per share on the 100 shares he had bought. How much did he receive in all?

Answer _____

2. Myron Nelson bought 90 shares of stock at $100 each. Three years later, he sold the stock for $95 per share. How much money did he lose?

Answer _____

3. Rose Wentworth owns 50 shares of stock in an oil company. The total number of shares of stock owned by all the stockholders in the company is 5000. What fraction of the shares does Rose own?

Answer _____

4. If the oil company declares dividends totaling $25,400, how much will Rose Wentworth receive in dividends?

Answer _____

5. Bob's mother gave him 10 shares of stock in a local company. She paid $52 per share for them. At the end of the first year, the company paid a dividend of $2.90 per share. How much did Bob receive in dividends?

Answer _____

6. The second year, Bob received $3.25 per share in dividends. How much more money did Bob receive the second year than the first year?

Answer _____

HANDLING MONEY

Single-Payment Loans

At a bank, some of the money that is deposited by customers in their savings accounts is used for loans to other customers. The bank *earns* interest from borrowers, but *pays* interest to depositors. The bank, of course, must charge a higher rate of interest on loans than it pays on savings accounts. Otherwise it could not make enough money to stay in business.

A **single-payment** loan is one that is repaid with one payment after a specified period of time. Interest on a single-payment loan is figured using the simple interest formula, $I = p \times r \times t$. If the loan is for more than a year, the customer may be required to pay the interest each year.

EXAMPLE   Jason Williams borrowed $560 from a bank to remodel his family room. The loan was for 4 months at 12% interest. How much interest did he pay? Remember to write the time as a number of years.

Principal		Rate (12%)		Time $\left(\frac{4}{12}\right)$		Interest
$560	$\times$	0.12	$\times$	0.333	=	$22.38

Complete each row of the chart.

	Principal	Rate	Time in Months	Time in Years	$p \times r \times t$ = Interest
1.	$500	8%	6	$\frac{1}{2}$ or 0.5	$500 × 0.08 × 0.5 =
2.	$820	12%	12		
3.	$1300	9%	3		
4.	$1530	10%	4		
5.	$2100	11%	18		
6.	$5900	10%	9		

7. Kathy borrowed $250 at 18% interest for 6 months. How much interest did she pay?

Answer _____

8. Molly Evans borrowed $1250 at 13% interest for 6 months. How much interest would she owe on the loan?

Answer _____

9. Harold Bowland borrowed $500 from the bank at 11% interest for 8 months. Including interest, how much did he have to repay?

Answer _____

10. A rancher borrowed $6000 from the bank for 4 months and agreed to pay 12% interest. Including interest, how much did he have to repay?

Answer _____

PROBLEM-SOLVING STRATEGY

Use Estimation

Many problems can be solved by estimation. Often, you do not need an exact answer to solve a problem. An estimate is found by rounding some or all of the numbers and then doing mental math.

Read the problem.

Ernest deposited $380 in a savings account that has an interest rate of 5.2%. About how much interest will be earned in 2 years?

Identify the important facts.

P = $380, r = 5.2% or 0.052, t = 2

Round.

Round $380 to $400 and round 5.2% to 5%.

Solve the problem.

Principal		Rate		Time		Interest
$400	×	0.05	×	2	=	$40

In two years, about $40 interest will be earned.

Use estimation to solve each problem.

---

1. Norman deposited $865 in a savings account that has an interest rate of 5.8%. About how much interest will be earned in 6 months?

Answer _____

2. Winona had a balance of $614 in her checking account. Then she deposited $385 and wrote a check for $423. Estimate the new balance.

Answer _____

---

3. Here are the amounts someone spent for groceries during a 3-week period.
$93 $78 $95
About how much money should be budgeted each week for groceries?

Answer _____

4. Hubert deposited $387 in a savings account at 7% interest. At this interest rate, the deposit will double in about 10 years. About how much money will be in the account in 10 years?

Answer _____

Use estimation to solve each problem.

5. Helen deposited $723 in a savings account at 5% interest. At this interest rate, the deposit will double in about 14 years. About how much money will be in the account in 14 years?

Answer _____

6. To find the number of years during which an investment to double in value, divide 70% by the interest rate. In about how many years will an investment double if the interest rate is 9.8%?

Answer _____

7. Cindy invested $1500 in a 2-year certificate that earns 8.34% interest. About how much interest will she receive on the investment?

Answer _____

8. Philip invested $3200 in a 6-month certificate of deposit that earns 7.75% interest. About how much interest will he receive on his investment?

Answer _____

9. The Rossi family has a monthly budget of $2300. Last month 19.8% of the budget was spent for food. About how much money was spent for food?

Answer _____

10. The Tyler family has a monthly budget of $1780. Last month 32% of the budget was spent for housing and utilities. About how much money was spent for housing and utilities?

Answer _____

11. Elinor owns 39 shares of stock. She received dividends of $2.05 per share. About how much did she receive in all?

Answer _____

12. Lewis owns 806 shares of stock. He received dividends of $0.87 per share. About how much money did he receive in all?

Answer _____

Installment Loans: Monthly Payments

Recall that a single-payment loan is repaid as a lump sum with interest. Most people find it easier to repay a loan with monthly payments, called **installments.** The table at the right can be used to find the amount of each monthly payment.

Businesses sometimes allow customers to pay for purchases with monthly installments. A lender or business that offers installment loans must inform borrowers of the interest rate, called the **annual percentage rate** or APR.

Monthly Payment per $100			
APR	6 mo	12 mo	18 mo
8%	$17.06	$8.70	$5.92
10%	$17.16	$8.79	$6.01
12%	$17.26	$8.89	$6.10
14%	$17.36	$8.98	$6.19
16%	$17.46	$9.07	$6.29
18%	$17.56	$9.16	$6.39

EXAMPLE Martha Conners bought a stereo for $940. She made a $140 down payment. The store offered to lend her the balance. She decides to repay the loan in 18 monthly installments. If the APR for the loan is 18%, how much is each monthly payment?

Cost		Down payment		Amount of loan
$940	−	$140	=	$800

Payment per $100		Loan in hundreds		Monthly payment
$6.39	×	8	=	$51.12

Each monthly payment is $51.12.

Find the monthly payment. Use information from the table of monthly payments.

	Amount	APR	Months	Payment
1.	$100	10%	6	
2.	$400	14%	6	
3.	$900	18%	12	
4.	$1400	12%	18	

	Amount	APR	Months	Payment
5.	$350	8%	18	
6.	$620	16%	12	
7.	$1700	14%	12	
8.	$4900	10%	18	

9. Mrs. Newhouse bought a tent for $150. She made a down payment of $50 and paid the balance in 12 monthly installments. If the APR was 16%, how much was each installment?

10. Matt bought a $2400 used car with a down payment of $800. He paid the balance in 6 monthly installments. If the APR was 12%, how much was each installment?

Answer _____

Answer _____

Installment Loans: Total Interest

To find the total interest on an installment loan, multiply the number of months by the amount paid each month. Then subtract the amount borrowed.

EXAMPLE How much interest is paid on a $3000 installment loan at 18%? The loan is to be repaid in 6 installments. The table on page 92 shows that the payment per $100 is $17.56.

Monthly payment: 30 (Loan in hundreds) × $17.56 = $526.80
Total of 6 payments: 6 × $526.80 = $3160.80
Total interest: $3160.80 − $3000 = $160.80

Complete each row of the chart.

	Amount of Loan	Interest (APR)	Number of Months	Monthly Payment	Total of Payments	Total Interest
1.	$200	14%	6	$34.72		
2.	$500	12%	12	$44.45		
3.	$1100	16%	18	$69.19		
4.	$2300	10%	12	$202.17		

Part of each installment is interest and the rest is applied to the principal, or amount owed. Because the amount owed on the loan decreases each month, the interest each month also decreases. This is shown by the payment schedule at the right. The amounts shown have been rounded.

Payment Schedule 6-Month Installment Loan of $3000, 18% Interest				
Payment Number	Payment	Interest Paid	Principal Paid	Balance $3000
1	$527	$45	$482	$2518
2	$527	$38	$489	$2029
3	$527	$31	$496	$1533
4	$527	$24	$503	$1030
5	$527	$16	$511	$519
6	$527	$8	$519	0

Answer each question about the payment schedule at the right.

5. For each payment, what is the sum of the interest paid and the principal paid?

Answer _____

6. What is the sum of the amounts in the column for *Principal Paid?*

Answer _____

7. What is the sum of the amounts in the column for *Interest Paid?*

Answer _____

8. How much interest would be paid on a single-payment loan of $3000 at 18% for 6 months? Will less interest be paid for a single-payment loan or an installment loan?

Answer _____

HANDLING MONEY
Credit Cards

A credit card allows you to pay less than the full amount you owe each month. But when you do not pay the full amount, you must pay a finance charge. This charge is found by multiplying the unpaid balance by the monthly interest rate, which is $\frac{1}{12}$ of the annual interest rate.

EXAMPLE   Arnold's unpaid balance on his credit card is $340. This month he made a payment of $70 and charged purchases totaling $175.78. The finance rate is 18% per year or 1.5% per month. What is his new balance?

Old balance	Payment	Balance after payment
$340	− $70	= $270

Rate	Balance after payment	Finance charge
0.015 ×	$270	= $4.05

To find the new balance, add the finance charge, $4.05, and new purchases, $175.78, to the balance after payment.

New balance: $270 + $4.05 + $175.78 = $449.83

Solve.

1. Mark's unpaid balance for last month was $258. He made a payment of $50 and did not use his credit card this month. What is the amount on which he will be charged a finance charge?

Answer _____

2. If the finance rate on Mark's credit card is 2% per month, what will be his finance charge on the unpaid balance?

Answer _____

3. If a department store credit card has a finance rate of 1.5% per month, what will be the finance charge on an unpaid balance of $560.80?

Answer _____

4. Angela has an unpaid balance of $320 on her credit card. The finance rate is 1.5% per month. If she makes a payment of $50 and does not make any new purchases, what will be her new balance?

Answer _____

5. Mr. Martinelli's unpaid balance is $300. If he makes a payment of $75 and buys an airplane ticket for $220, what will be his new balance? The finance rate is 1% per month.

Answer _____

6. Dr. Wong's credit card has a finance rate of 2% per month. Her unpaid balance is $1600. If she makes a payment of $40 and buys a table for $150, what will be her new balance?

Answer _____

Unit 4 Review

Solve.

1. Phyllis has a yearly income of $26,000. She budgets 15% for clothing. How much will she have for clothing?

   Answer _____

2. One month, Georgia earned $350. She spent $125 for rent, $45 for food, and $70 for miscellaneous items. How much did she have left to put into her savings account?

   Answer _____

3. Agnes has a balance in her checking account of $450.70. If she writes a check for $35.15 and makes a deposit of $120.40, what will her new balance be?

   Answer _____

4. Bill deposited $520 in a savings account that pays 6% simple interest per year. How much interest will he earn in 1 year?

   Answer _____

5. Frances puts $1200 into a savings account that pays 6% interest, compounded annually. How much will she have in the account in 2 years?

   Answer _____

6. Barbara buys three $100 U.S. savings bonds for $50 each. A $100 bond will be worth $90.32 in 10 years. How much will Barbara's bonds be worth in 10 years?

   Answer _____

7. Bob has $6000 in a 1-year CD at 7% interest. How much interest will he receive at the end of 1 year?

   Answer _____

8. A farmer borrowed $13,000 for 6 months at 11% interest. How much interest will he pay on the loan?

   Answer _____

9. Ronnie borrowed $1500 to buy a computer. He will repay the loan in 12 installments of $134.70 each. How much interest will he pay on the loan?

   Answer _____

10. Susan has an unpaid balance on her credit card of $450. If the finance rate is 2% per month, what is the finance charge on her balance?

    Answer _____

Buying a New Car: Sticker Price

Buying a new car requires careful consideration of various costs. At the factory, a sticker is put on a new car to show the suggested sales price. The **sticker price** includes the base price of the car plus the cost of special equipment (options) plus the cost of shipping the car from the factory to the dealer (destination charge). The costs for sales tax and license fees are *not* included on the sticker and are added later.

A customer ordered a Sparky with power windows, air conditioning, and power brakes. Use prices from the chart to find the sticker price.

Option costs: $145 + $615 + $84 = $844
Sticker price: $6580 + $844 + $278 = $7702

SPARKY (Compact Car)	
BASE PRICE	$6580
OPTIONS:	
Power windows	$145
Automatic transmission	$599
Air conditioning	$615
Power brakes	$84
Tinted glass	$75
Cruise control	$120
DESTINATION CHARGE	$278

Solve. For Exercises 1 and 2, refer to the chart above.

1. A customer orders a Sparky with automatic transmission and air conditioning. What is the sticker price?

Answer _____

2. A customer orders a Sparky with all six of the options that are listed. What is the sticker price?

Answer _____

3. A customer orders a minivan with these options: automatic transmission, $724; power steering, $329; and cruise control, $134. What is the total cost of options?

Answer _____

4. The minivan from Exercise 3 has a base price of $10,941 and destination charge of $345. What is the sticker price?

Answer _____

5. The base price of an Encore TZ is $9052. The customer has selected options that have a total cost of $713. The destination charge is $250. What is the sticker price?

Answer _____

6. The base price of a conversion van is $13,108. The customer selects options that cost $859. The destination charge is $265. What is the sticker price?

Answer _____

Buying a New Car: Dealer's Cost

The dealer's cost of buying the car from the factory is usually 75% to 80% of the sticker price. A customer might save money by offering a price that is between the sticker price and the dealer's cost.

Consumer magazines often give reports of the dealer's cost for a car. For the Sparky the dealer pays 78% of the base price, 75% of the cost of options, and all of the destination charge.

How much does the dealer pay for a Sparky with power windows, air conditioning, and power brakes? Would $7100 be a reasonable offer? For each step, round the amount to the nearest dollar.

Dealer's cost:
78% of base price = $0.78 \times \$6580 =$ $5132
75% of options = $0.75 \times \$844 =$ 633
Destination charge =   +278
      $6043

The offer of $7100 seems reasonable. However, if there is high demand for the car, the dealer may not agree to sell for less than the sticker price.

Solve. Round to the nearest dollar.

1. A dealer buys a small station wagon with no options. The dealer's cost is 78% of the base price of $9588, plus a destination charge of $285. Find the dealer's cost.

   Answer _____

2. For the station wagon in Exercise 1, what is the difference between the sticker price and the dealer's cost?

   Answer _____

3. The dealer's cost for a fullsize car includes 82% of the base price of $14,560 and 78% of the options cost of $2148. The dealer's cost also includes a destination charge of $357. What is the dealer's cost?

   Answer _____

4. The dealer's cost for a midsize car includes 78% of the base price of $11,099 and 75% of the options cost of $1343. The dealer's cost also includes a destination charge of $277. What is the dealer's cost?

   Answer _____

5. For the fullsize car in Exercise 3, the dealer accepts an offer that is 10% less than the sticker price. How much does the customer pay for the car?

   Answer _____

6. For the midsize car in Exercise 4, the dealer accepts an offer that is $1300 less than the sticker price. How much does the customer pay for the car?

   Answer _____

Buying a Used Car

A person who is buying a used car may save money by offering less than the asking price. This is because car dealers often set prices that are higher than what they expect to get. After a car buyer makes an offer, the dealer will probably adjust the price to an amount between the offer and the original price. So, wise buyers often make offers that are less than what they expect to pay.

Monthly consumer guides list the average prices for used cars bought from dealers during the previous month. This information can help a car buyer decide how much to offer for a used car. The chart lists the dealer's price and the guidebook's price for the used cars at a certain dealer.

Used Car Model	Dealer Price	Guide Price
Caravan	$7000	$6500
Royale	$4200	$4425
Imperial	$9595	$7850
Horizon	$3400	$2675
Mustang	$8498	$6200
Sprint	$999	$700

For the Imperial, Rene offered $200 less than the guidebook's price. The dealer lowered the price of the car by $1195 and Rene agreed to the new price. How much was her offer? What price was agreed on?

Rene's offer: $7850 − $200 = $7650
Agreement price: $9595 − $1195 = $8400

Solve. Use prices from the chart.

1. Find the difference between the dealer's price and the guidebook's price for each model.

   Caravan _____   Royale _____

   Imperial _____   Horizon _____

   Mustang _____   Sprint _____

2. For which used car is the guidebook's price higher than the dealer's price? Suppose a customer offers $3800 for that car. How much less is the offer than the guidebook's price?

   Answer _____

3. A customer offers the dealer $5900 for the Caravan. The dealer and customer reach agreement on a price that is $800 less than the dealer's original price. How much does the customer pay?

   Answer _____

4. For the Mustang, a customer offers the dealer the guidebook's price. The dealer is willing to sell for $500 more than that. How much is the dealer willing to reduce his asking price?

   Answer _____

5. Suppose you offer 10% less than the dealer's price for the Horizon. How much is your offer?

   Answer _____

6. Suppose you will pay 10% more than the guidebook's price for the Sprint. How much will you pay?

   Answer _____

DRIVING A CAR

Renting a Car

If a person only needs a car occasionally, it may be less expensive to rent than to buy. A car rental company usually has daily or weekly rates. Some companies also charge an additional amount for the mileage. The chart at the right shows the rates at Carla's Car Rental.

Carla's Car Rental		
Type	Daily Rate*	Weekly Rate*
Compact	$26.95	$169.00
Mid-size	$32.95	$199.00
Full-Size	$39.95	$239.00
Van for 8	$45.95	$259.00
*150 free miles per day. Add $0.20 for each additional mile.		

Norman Riley rented a mid-size car for 2 days and drove 358 miles. How many miles will he be charged for? How much was the rental cost?

Total miles	Free miles (150 × 2)	Chargeable miles
358 −	300 =	58

Basic charge 2 × $32.95	Additional charge 58 × $0.20	Rental cost
$65.90 +	$11.60 =	$77.50

Complete each row of the table using prices from Carla's Car Rental. The first row is a sample based on the example above.

	Customer's Name	Type of Car	Length of Rental	Miles Driven	Rate (see above)	Basic Charge	Chargeable Miles	Additional Charge	Rental Cost
	N. Riley	Mid-size	2 days	358	$32.95	$65.90	58	$11.60	$77.50
1.	M. Wilson	Compact	2 days	195					
2.	R. Edwards	Mid-size	2 weeks	1295					
3.	B. Quigley	Van	5 days	1024					
4.	S. Schott	Van	3 days	764					
5.	S. Lee	Full-size	1 week	1500					

6. Milton Anderson wants to rent a compact car for 16 days. How many weeks and days is this? How much is the basic charge at Carla's Car Rental for that length of time? If 8% sales tax is added, how much is the total charge?

7. Liz Thompson does not own a car. She rents a compact car about 6 days per month, and drives less than 150 miles each time. How much does she spend each month for rental costs? Would she save money by buying a new car that would require payments of $250 per month?

Answer _____

Answer _____

DRIVING A CAR

Financing a Car: Monthly Payment

Once you have decided which car to buy and where to buy it, you need to decide where to borrow the money to pay for it. You can finance the car through the dealer or borrow money from a bank or finance company. Most banks do not lend the full price of a car. If you trade-in an older car, the dealer gives you a **trade-in allowance** that may serve as a down payment.

Usually a new car loan is for 3 years or more. Sometimes you can get a lower interest rate if you take out a loan for a shorter period of time. The table at the right can be used to find monthly payments. What is the monthly payment on a $9200 loan for 4 years at 12%?

The payment is $2.63 per $100. So, the payment for a $9200 loan is 92 × $2.63 or $241.96.

Monthly Payment per $100			
Int. Rate	3 yr	4 yr	5 yr
11%	$3.27	$2.59	$2.18
12%	$3.32	$2.63	$2.22
13%	$3.37	$2.68	$2.27
14%	$3.42	$2.73	$2.33
15%	$3.47	$2.78	$2.38
16%	$3.52	$2.83	$2.43

Find the monthly payment. Use information from the table of monthly payments.

	Amount	Int. Rate	Years	Payment
1.	$4400	13%	4	
2.	$2000	14%	3	
3.	$6200	11%	4	
4.	$1800	14%	3	

	Amount	Int. Rate	Years	Payment
5.	$3500	12%	3	
6.	$7900	16%	5	
7.	$5100	15%	5	
8.	$8900	12%	4	

9. Sarah buys a car for $11,385. She has no car to trade in. Her down payment is $1385. If she takes out a loan at 13% interest for 5 years, how much will the monthly payments be?

Answer _____

10. Morris buys a car for $10,295. He gets a trade-in allowance of $2295 for his old car. If he takes out a loan at 12% interest for 4 years, how much will the monthly payments be?

Answer _____

11. Suppose Sarah decides to take out a loan at 12% interest for 3 years. How much will the monthly payments be? (See Exercise 9.)

Answer _____

12. Suppose Morris gets $500 more for the trade-in allowance. How much will the monthly payments be? (See Exercise 10.)

Answer _____

100

Financing a Car: Total Interest Paid

The monthly payment on a 4-year loan of $9200 at 12% is $241.96. How much interest will be paid on the loan?

First find the number of months in 4 years.

$$4 \times 12 = 48$$

Then multiply the number of months by the amount paid each month, and subtract the amount borrowed.

$48 \times \$241.96 = \$11,614.08$
$\$11614.08 - \$9200 = \$2414.08$ Total interest

Monthly Payment per $100			
Int. Rate	3 yr	4 yr	5 yr
11%	$3.27	$2.59	$2.18
12%	$3.32	$2.63	$2.22
13%	$3.37	$2.68	$2.27
14%	$3.42	$2.73	$2.33
15%	$3.47	$2.78	$2.38
16%	$3.52	$2.83	$2.43

Complete each row of the chart. For rows 5 and 6, use the table to find the monthly payments.

	Amount of Loan	Interest Rate	Number of Years	Monthly Payment	Total of Payments	Total interest
1.	$10,000	13%	5	$227.00		
2.	$10,000	11%	5	$233.00		
3.	$8,000	15%	3	$277.60		
4.	$8,000	15%	5	$190.40		
5.	$4900	13%	4			
6.	$5500	11%	3			

7. Exercises 1 and 2 above differ only by the interest rate. How much less total interest will be paid if the interest rate is 13% instead of 14%?

Answer _____

8. Exercises 3 and 4 above differ only by the number of years. How much less total interest will be paid on the 3-year loan than the 5-year loan?

Answer _____

9. Morris buys a car for $14,295. He makes a down payment of $1295. If he takes out a loan at 12% interest for 4 years, how much will the monthly payments be?

Answer _____

10. Refer to Exercise 9. What will be the total of the monthly payments? What will be the total cost of the car, including interest?

Answer _____

DRIVING A CAR

Automobile Insurance: Base Premiums

Insurance is another large expense of operating a car. The cost is based on the sex and age of the driver, the size and value of the car, where the car is driven, and other factors. A car owner buys an **insurance policy** and pays **premiums** to an insurance company. The company then agrees to pay certain accident costs. Some policies have a **deductible clause.** A $100-deductible clause means that the insured person pays the first $100 of the repair bill, and the insurance company pays the rest.

The chart at the right shows the **base premiums** that one company charges for collision and comprehensive insurance. **Collision insurance** pays to repair the insured person's car after an accident. **Comprehensive insurance** pays to repair the car in case of fire, theft, or damage caused by storms.

Car Type	YEARLY BASE PREMIUM			
	Collision		Comprehensive	
	$100Ded.	$250Ded.	$50Ded.	$100Ded.
A	$109.30	$79.40	$42.20	$31.40
B	120.50	111.60	62.10	47.30
C	134.70	162.50	78.30	59.90

What is the total yearly base premium for each of these policies? (Hint: Find the base premium for each amount of insurance and add.)

1. Car Type A, Collision with $250 deductible, Comprehensive with $50 deductible. _____

2. Car Type C, Collision with $250 deductible, Comprehensive with $100 deductible _____

3. Car Type B, Collision with $100 deductible, Comprehensive with $50 deductible. _____

4. Car Type A, Collision with $100 deductible, Comprehensive with $100 deductible. _____

In addition to collision and comprehensive insurance, many states require drivers to buy **liability insurance** of the following types. **Property damage insurance** pays to repair the damages to other people's cars or property. **Bodily injury insurance** pays for medical expenses after an accident.

The chart at the right shows annual base premiums charged by one company. A bodily injury limit of 50/100 means that the insurance company will pay up to $50,000 to each person injured, with a limit of $100,000 if more than one person is injured.

Yearly Base Premiums for Liability Insurance			
Bodily Injury Limits	Premium	Property Damage Limits	Premium
50/100	145.20	$25,000	$55.20
100/300	$160.80	$50,000	$59.30
250/500	$168.10	$100,000	$64.80

What is the total yearly base premium for each of these liability insurance policies? (Hint: Find the base premium for each amount of insurance and add.)

5. Bodily injury 100/300 Property damage $25,000 _____

6. Bodily injury 50/100 property damage $100,000 _____

7. Bodily injury 250/500 Property damage $50,000 _____

8. Bodily injury 100/300 Property damage $50,000 _____

Automobile Insurance: Driver-Rating Factor

After an insurance company finds the base premium for a policy, this amount is multiplied by the **driver-rating factor**. A person with a high driver-rating factor pays much more for insurance than a person with a low driver-rating factor. An insurance company may use a table like the one at the right to determine the driver-rating factor for an unmarried person. The factor would be lower for a married person and higher for someone who has had previous accidents.

DRIVER-RATING FACTORS FOR UNMARRIED PRINCIPAL OPERATORS		
MALES	**For Pleasure**	**For Work**
Under age 21	3.9	4.1
Age 21-24	2.9	3.1
Age 25-29	1.7	1.9
FEMALES	**For Pleasure**	**For Work**
Under age 21	1.8	2.0
Age 21-24	1.6	1.8
Age 25-29	1.0	1.2

Larry is an unmarried male, age 22, who drives for pleasure. What is Larry's driver-rating factor? How much will Larry pay for an insurance policy that has a base premium of $245 per year?

Larry's driver-rating factor is 2.9.
2.9 × $245 = $710.50.
The policy will cost $710.50.

Use the table above to find the driver-rating factor for each person. Then find the total annual premium.

	Driver Description	Rating Factor	Annual Base Premium	Total Annual Premium
1.	25-year old unmarried female who drives for work		$183.90	
2.	19-year old unmarried male who drives for work		$207.70	
3.	18-year old unmarried female who drives for work		$152.40	
4.	28-year old unmarried male who drives for pleasure		$139.05	

Use the tables on page 102 to answer each question.

5. Marilyn Lee has a driver-rating factor of 2.0 and drives a type B car. What is her yearly premium for this policy?

- Bodily injury with limit of 50/100
- Property damage with limit of $50,000
- Collision with $250 deductible
- Comprehensive with $100 deductible

Answer _____

6. Jon Carlson has a driver-rating factor of 2.5 and drives a type C car. What is his yearly premium for this policy?

- Bodily injury with limit of 100/300
- Property damage with limit of $100,000
- Comprehensive with $50 deductible
- Collision with $100 deductible

Answer _____

DRIVING A CAR

Miles per Gallon

To find a car's gasoline mileage, divide the number of miles traveled by the number of gallons of gasoline used.

Jeff Sims kept a log book of his gasoline purchases. He always fills the tank. On January 31 he bought 16.2 gallons of gasoline for $22.52. How many miles did he travel between January 24 and January 31?

Date	Odometer	Gallons	Cost
1/24	42,891	Full	
1/31	43,293	16.2	$22.52
2/4	43,603	13.5	$19.58
2/10	44,010	15.8	$23.49
2/15	44,267	11.4	$16.85

$$43,293 - 42,891 = 402 \text{ miles}$$

What was the gas mileage in miles per gallon (mpg)? Divide the number of miles traveled by the number of gallons used. Round the quotient to the nearest whole number.

$$402 \text{ miles} \div 16.2 \text{ gallons} = 24.81 \text{ or } 25 \text{ mpg}$$

What was the cost of gasoline per mile? Divide $22.52 by the number of miles driven. Round the quotient to three decimal places.

$$\$22.52 \div 402 = \$0.056 \text{ or } 5.6\cent \text{ per mile}$$

Complete each row of the table. Use data from the chart above.

	Date of Gasoline Purchase	Miles Traveled Since Last Purchase	Miles per Gallon	Cost per Mile (in cents)
1.	February 4			
2.	February 10			
3.	February 15			

---

4. Bart's car used 26 gallons of gasoline in 780 miles. How many miles per gallon was this?

Answer _____

5. Joy's car used 12.6 gallons of gasoline in 288 miles. How many miles per gallon was this?

Answer _____

---

6. Suppose gasoline costs $1.23 per gallon and you use 24 gallons per week. How much would you need to spend for gasoline each week?

Answer _____

7. Teresa took a 540-mile trip. She used 19 gallons of gasoline and paid $1.28 per gallon. What was the cost per mile for gasoline?

Answer _____

Mileage Table

If you have used a road map, you may have seen a mileage table like the one at the right. Before a trip is begun, the wise motorist will find out the distances so that she or he can make plans accordingly.

To find the mileage between two cities, find one of the cities in the left-hand column. Lay a ruler along that row to the column headed by the other city's name. Find the road distance from Atlanta to New York.

Atlanta is the first city in the left column. Move along that row to the column for New York. The distance is 868 miles.

AUTOMOBILE MILEAGE	Chicago, Ill.	Denver, Colo.	Houston, Tex.	Los Angeles, Calif.	Miami, Fla.	New York, N.Y.	San Francisco, Calif.
Atlanta, Ga.	671	1436	852	2245	663	868	2579
Boston, Mass.	992	2016	1865	3004	1615	220	3265
Chicago, Ill.		1062	1139	2115	1352	824	2240
Cleveland, Ohio	311	1393	1372	2393	1327	493	2571
Dallas, Tex.	923	820	241	1476	1367	1580	1790
Denver, Colo.	1062		1061	1148	2104	1794	1324
Detroit, Mich.	271	1333	1306	2415	1437	670	2511
Houston, Tex.	1139	1061		1585	1256	1714	1950
Las Vegas, Nev.	1905	843	1426	305	2572	2637	624
Los Angeles, Calif.	2115	1148	1585		2841	2784	411
Memphis, Tenn.	579	1054	560	1816	1050	1114	2214
Miami, Fla.	1352	2104	1256	2841		1395	3192
Montreal, Quebec	804	1866	1839	2948	1749	381	3044
New Orleans, La.	981	1326	360	1945	896	1360	2296
New York, N.Y.	824	1794	1714	2784	1395		3045
Philadelphia, Pa.	766	1770	1624	2726	1278	90	3021
Portland, Oreg.	2255	1329	2295	1098	3433	2992	687
St. Louis, Mo.	293	840	856	1832	1346	1057	2168
Seattle, Wash.	2076	1411	2377	1280	3421	2852	869
Toronto, Ontario	469	1531	1504	2613	1631	513	2709
Washington, D.C.	701	1696	1476	2680	1130	238	2968

1. How far is it from Atlanta to Los Angeles? _____

2. How far is it from Boston to San Francisco? _____

3. From Chicago to Los Angeles is how many miles by road? _____

4. From Detroit to New York is how far? _____

5. How far is it from Denver to Philadelphia? (It does not make any difference which one of the cities is in the left-hand column and which is at the top. The distance between the two cities is the same, in either direction.)

6. Margaret and her family took a trip by car from Miami to Memphis. How many miles is this? _____

7. The average speed for the trip was 50 miles per hour. How many driving hours did it take to make the trip? _____

8. They averaged 28 miles to the gallon of gasoline. How many gallons did they use? _____

9. At an average price of $1.48 a gallon, how much did the gas for the trip cost? _____

10. The Fontaine family drove from Montreal to Miami. How many miles is this? _____

11. They averaged 30 miles to the gallon of gas on the trip. How many gallons did they use? _____

12. At $1.53 a gallon on the average, how much did the gas cost? _____

13. How far is it from Houston to Las Vegas? _____

PROBLEM-SOLVING STRATEGY
Work Backwards

Sometimes you are told what happened at the end of a problem and asked to find what happened at the beginning. You can find the solution to a problem like this by working backwards.

Read the problem.

The final sales price of a new car was $9849. This price included sticker price, $555 tax, and a $44 license fee. What was the sticker price?

Use the strategy.

Sticker price + Tax + License fee = Final price
  ???   + $555 + $44   = $9849

To find the sticker price, work backwards from the final price of $9849. Undo each operation by using the inverse operation. For example, you would use subtraction to undo addition. (You would use division to undo multiplication.)

$9849 − $44 − $555 = Sticker price

First subtract $44. $9849 − $44 = $9805
Then subtract $555. $9805 − $555 = $9250

The sticker price was $9250.

Solve by working backwards.

---

1. A used car dealer agreed to reduce the price of a used car to $2300. This was $599 less than the dealer's original price. How much was the original price?

Answer _____

2. A customer ordered a car that had a sticker price of $13,721. This included the base price of $11,939, destination charge of $309, and several options. What was the total cost of the options?

Answer _____

3. A customer ordered a car that had a sticker price of $8350. The sticker price included options totaling $1285 and a destination charge of $249. What was the base price?

Answer _____

4. Marla rented a car and was charged a total of $63.96. This included a basic charge of $49.00 plus an additional charge for 68 miles. How much was she charged for each additional mile?

Answer _____

Solve.

5. Bradley rented a car and was charged a total of $105.05. He paid for 3 days at the daily rate plus $6.20 for additional miles. What was the daily rate for renting the car?

Answer _____

6. Greg borrowed for a car and is making payments of $147.15 per month for 36 months. When he finishes paying off the loan, he will have paid a total of $797.40 in interest. What was the amount of the loan?

Answer _____

7. The total base premium for Eugene's two types of liability insurance is $215.30. The base premium for bodily injury insurance is $131.90. What is the base premium for the property damage insurance?

Answer _____

8. Yolanda Everett has a driver-rating factor of 1.8. Her total annual premium for car insurance is $388.80. What is the annual base premium?

Answer _____

9. When Paula Pearson bought gasoline on March 8, the odometer reading was 34,901. This was 329 more than the odometer reading on March 1. What was the odometer reading on March 1?

Answer _____

10. Oscar bought a road map and 12.5 gallons of gasoline for $20.50. The road map cost $2.00. What was the price per gallon of gasoline?

Answer _____

Calculator Applications

Some problems require more than one operation. Suppose you use a calculator to find the value of 549 − 36 × 8, as shown at the right.

Standard Calculator

549 ⊟ 36 ⊠ 8 ⊟ ▭ 4104.

Why are there two different answers? A standard calculator does the operations one at a time as they are entered. A scientific calculator does multiplication and division before addition and subtraction. Which type of calculator do you have?

Scientific Calculator

549 ⊟ 36 ⊠ 8 ⊟ ▭ 261.

Since 549 − 36 × 8 should have only one value, parentheses are used to show which operation to do first. Which calculator found the value of (549 − 36) × 8? Which calculator found the value of 549 − (36 × 8)?

If you are using a scientific calculator and you want it to complete an operation, press ⊟ before entering the next operation.

EXAMPLE When Maxwell filled the gas tank of his car, the odometer reading was 14,285. When he filled the tank previously, the reading was 13,977. He bought 10.4 gallons of gas. What is the car's gas mileage?

Find the value of (14,285 − 13,977) ÷ 10.4

14285 ⊟ 13977 ⊟ ⊟ 10.4 ⊟ ▭ 29.615384

The gas mileage is 29.6 miles per gallon.

Use a calculator to find each value. Round to the nearest tenth.

1. 984.2 − (845 ÷ 5) _____

2. (984.2 − 845) ÷ 5 _____

3. 1000 ÷ (14.6 + 8.4) _____

4. (1000 ÷ 14.6) + 8.4 _____

5. $8392 − ($530 + $239) _____

6. ($8392 − $530) + $539 _____

Solve.

7. When Jenny filled the gas tank of her car, the odometer reading was 58,513. When she filled the tank previously, the reading was 58,216. She bought 12.3 gallons of gas. What is the car's gas mileage?

8. When Dave filled the gas tank of his car, the odometer reading was 25,542. He bought 9.7 gallons of gas and figured the gas mileage was about 33 miles per gallon. What was the odometer reading when he filled the car with gas previously?

Answer _____

Answer _____

DRIVING A CAR

Depreciation

The value of a car goes down every year. This decrease in value is called **depreciation.** A new car depreciates most during the first year. Then it depreciates at a slower rate. Some cars depreciate more quickly than others. Guidebooks that list used car values can be helpful in finding out how much a car has depreciated, and, therefore, how much it is worth at the time.

Depreciation is often given as a percent of the purchase price. The approximate trade-in or sale value of a car can be found by subtracting the amount of depreciation from the car's purchase price.

The purchase price of a new car was $8500. In the first year, its value depreciated 30%. In the second year, its value depreciated 15%. Find the amount of depreciation each year and the approximate trade-in or sale value after two years.

First year depreciation 30% of $8500	Second year depreciation 15% of $8500	Approximate trade-in or sale value after 2 years
$0.30 \times \$8500 = \$2550$	$0.15 \times \$8500 = \$1275$	$\$8500 - \$2550 - \$1275 = \$4675$

The approximate trade-in or sale value after two years is $4675.

Find the amount of depreciation each year, for the given rates. Then find the approximate trade-in value after 4 years.

	Purchase Price of Car	Year 1 30%	Year 2 15%	Year 3 12%	Year 4 8%	Approximate Trade-In Value
1.	$10,000	$0.30 \times 10,000$				
2.	$12,430					
3.	$9820					
4.	$13,800					
5.	$6740					

6. If the value of a car depreciates $3000 in one year, what is the average depreciation per month? (Hint: Divide the amount by the number of months in a year.)

7. The trade-in value of Ruth Gorman's car is $3500. She purchased the car for $8180 and has had it for 36 months. What was the average amount of depreciation per month?

Answer _____

Answer _____

DRIVING A CAR

Car Maintenance

Another expense of operating a car is maintenance to keep the car in good running condition. Some items included in car maintenance are oil, oil filters, grease, fuel filters, spark plugs, and tires. Many people have their cars maintained by service stations, shops, or car dealers.

Ria Waterson had her car serviced at Red's Service Station. The **invoice,** or bill, at the right shows what work was done, how many hours of labor are being charged, and how much the parts cost. Study the amounts on the invoice. This is how to compute the total charge.

First, add to find the total number of hours of labor.

$$0.25 + 0.5 + 0.25 + 0.5 = 1.5 \text{ hours}$$

Add to find the total cost of the parts.

$$\$6.45 + \$16.00 + \$7.35 + \$3.85 = \$33.65$$

From the invoice you can see that the labor charge was $28.00 per hour. Multiply the hours by $28 to find the labor charge.

$$1.5 \text{ hours} \times \$28/\text{hour} = \$42$$

Add the labor charge to the parts charge.

$$\$33.65 + \$42.00 = \$75.65$$

RED'S SERVICE STATION		
Customer: name: *Ria Waterson*		
Auto license number: *MDY 330*		
Work done	**Hours**	**Parts**
Replace:		
Oil Filter	*0.25*	*$6.45*
Spark Plugs (set of 4)	*0.5*	*16.00*
Air Filter	*0.25*	*7.35*
Fuel Filter	*0.5*	*3.85*
Totals	*1.5*	*$33.65*
Labor charge: Number of Hours × 28.00 =		*$42.00*
Total Charge: Parts + Labor =		*$75.65*

Solve.

1. Complete the invoice form below to find the total charge.

PAT'S AUTO SERVICE		
Customer: *Henry Ruscilli*		
Auto license number: *GXR 498*		
Work done	**Hours**	**Parts**
Rotate Tires	*1.0*	*0*
Spark Plugs (set of 6)	*0.75*	*19.50*
Air Filter	*0.25*	*6.95*
Fuel Filter	*0.25*	*4.50*
Totals		
Labor charge: Number of Hours × 32.00 =		
Total Charge: Parts + Labor =		

2. A different customer at Red's Service Station above was charged for 3.25 total hours of labor. What was the labor charge?

Answer _____

3. A service station charges a total of $20.60 to change the oil and oil filter on Nathan's car. Nathan can buy an oil filter for $2.50 and the oil for $4.20 at a discount store. How much will he save if he does the work himself?

Answer _____

4. Vera took her car to a service station that charged $45.00 per hour for labor. If the invoice included $47 for parts and 2.5 hours for labor, what was the total charge?

Answer _____

Estimates for Car Repairs

Because cars are expensive to maintain and repair, a car owner needs to allow money in the budget to cover these costs. Also, a car owner should search for a reliable repair shop that has reasonable prices. One way to find a reliable shop is to ask friends and neighbors for references.

When major repairs are needed, the owner of a car may want to get estimates from two or three different shops. Three estimates for the same work are shown below.

Repair	ESTIMATES		
	Shop A	Shop B	Shop C
Replace brakes	$173.78	$251.00	$178.50
Align front end	20.00	16.88	18.45
Service air conditioning	19.88	23.35	21.66
Service transmission	32.50	26.78	28.50
Tune up engine (6 cyl)	49.65	38.44	39.88
TOTALS:			

1. Complete the table to find the total for the repairs at each shop.

2. Which shop has the lowest estimate for these repairs? How much less than the most expensive shop does it charge?

Answer _____

3. Which shop charges the least for replacing brakes? How much less than the most expensive shop does it charge?

Answer _____

4. How much would you save by having the transmission serviced at Shop B rather than at Shop A?

Answer _____

5. Suppose you want to have the brakes replaced and the engine tuned at the same shop. From which shop would you get the best price? How much would you pay at that shop?

Answer _____

6. Suppose you want to have the front end aligned and the transmission serviced at the same shop. What is the best price you could get?

Answer _____

7. Paul's car was in an accident and needed a new fender. Paul got three different estimates for repairs: $790, $912, and $944. Paul has a $200-deductible clause in his insurance coverage. The insurance company paid the lowest estimate, except for the deductible. How much was paid by the insurance company?

Answer _____

Public Transportation

Most cities have various kinds of public transportation, such as buses and trains. The companies that operate the public transportation often sell monthly passes in addition to single-ride tickets. If a person uses public transportation frequently, buying a monthly pass may be a way to save money. Riding buses or trains is usually less expensive than owning and operating a car.

Teresa Porter rides the train to work and back 22 days in a month. A single-ride ticket costs $0.90 and a monthly pass costs $28.50. How much money would she save by buying a monthly pass instead of single-ride tickets?

Single-ride ticket		Days per month		Rides per day		Total cost
$0.90	×	22	×	2	=	$39.60

Find the difference between $39.60 and $28.50.
She would save $11.10 each month.

Solve.

1. Suppose you ride a bus to and from work 24 days per month. A single-ride ticket costs $1.20. A monthly ticket costs $42.00. Which ticket will cost less to use each month? How much less?

Answer _____

2. Use the information in Exercise 1. Suppose you took a 5-day vacation in one month. Would you pay more or less if you bought a monthly ticket for that month? How much more or less?

Answer _____

3. Suppose you ride a train to and from work 20 days per month. A single-ride ticket costs $3.75. A monthly ticket costs $105.00. How much will you save each month by using a monthly pass?

Answer _____

4. Vernon drives to work some days and rides a bus other days. The bus costs $1.65 each way. When he drives, he pays $4.00 per day for parking and about $2.20 for gasoline. How much less does it cost each day to ride the bus?

Answer _____

5. Here is a fare schedule for a bus company.

	Monday-Friday	Saturday-Sunday
Adults	$1.50	$1.00
Children	$1.00	$0.75

How much will a family of 2 adults and 3 children pay for a round trip on a Monday?

Answer _____

6. Use information from Exercise 5. How much will the same family pay if they ride on a Saturday? How much less will they pay on Saturday than on Monday?

Answer _____

DRIVING A CAR

Airline Schedules

The table at the right is a sample airline schedule. It gives hours of departure and arrival, flight numbers, and number of stops. Note that the times are either central daylight time (CDT) or eastern daylight time (EDT).

Reggie Smolen has a ticket on flight 329 from Kansas City to Minneapolis. How much time is required for the flight?

Find flight 329 in the Kansas City to Minneapolis section of the table. Read across. The flight leaves at 7:45 P.M. and arrives at 9:40 P.M. The flight takes 1 hour and 55 minutes.

	Leave	Arrive	Flight	Stops
CHICAGO (CDT) to HOUSTON (CDT)	8:50 A.M.	2:47 P.M.	239	4-Stop
	2:40 P.M.	4:53 P.M.	531	Non-Stop
	7:15 P.M.	10:47 P.M.	68	1-Stop
	9:00 P.M.	12:22 A.M.	374	1-Stop
	11:20 P.M.	1:33 A.M.	286	Non-Stop
KANSAS CITY (CDT) TO MINNEAPOLIS (CDT)	7:25 A.M.	9:15 A.M.	169	1-Stop
	9:50 A.M.	10:56 A.M.	184	Non-Stop
	11:25 A.M.	1:20 P.M.	246	1-Stop
	2:15 P.M.	4:10 P.M.	381	1-Stop
	5:05 P.M.	6:11 P.M.	62	Non-Stop
	6:00 P.M.	7:55 P.M.	418	1-Stop
	7:45 P.M.	9:40 P.M.	329	1-Stop
	9:10 P.M.	10:16 P.M.	172	Non-Stop
	9:15 P.M.	10:59 P.M.	96	1-Stop
WASHINGTON (EDT) to MIAMI (EDT)	7:00 A.M.	11:30 A.M.	218	3-Stop
	8:05 A.M.	11:03 A.M.	8	1-Stop
	9:45 A.M.	12:01 P.M.	36	Non-Stop
	2:00 P.M.	4:13 P.M.	472	Non-Stop
	4:30 P.M.	6:45 P.M.	10	Non-Stop
	6:45 P.M.	8:57 P.M.	302	Non-Stop
	9:30 P.M.	12:43 A.M.	181	1-Stop

Note: Departing and arriving times are based on time zones in each city.

Use the airline schedule to answer each question.

1. Flight 329 makes 1 stop before arriving in Minneapolis. Look at flight 172. How much less time does the nonstop flight take?

   Answer _____

2. Mr. Bolten lives in Chicago. He has a ticket on the first afternoon plane to Houston. What time does the plane leave?

   Answer _____

3. What time will it be in Houston when Mr. Bolten arrives?

   Answer _____

4. How much time is required for flight 218 from Washington to Miami?

   Answer _____

5. If you take flight 36 instead of flight 218, how long will the trip take?

   Answer _____

6. How many stops does flight 239 from Chicago make before landing in Houston?

   Answer _____

7. Mrs. Templeton wants to fly from Kansas City to Minneapolis. She needs to arrive before 7 P.M. What is the flight number of the latest afternoon plane she can take?

   Answer _____

8. When will Mrs. Templeton arrive in Minneapolis?

   Answer _____

9. How much time is required for flight 62 from Kansas City to Minneapolis?

   Answer _____

10. How much more time does flight 418 take than flight 62?

   Answer _____

PROBLEM-SOLVING STRATEGY

Find a Pattern

By studying patterns, you may be able to solve problems or discover mistakes that have been made. When one number in a problem is changed, the result may change according to a certain pattern.

Read the problem.

Three different customers rented compact cars from the same rental company. This chart shows the length of time the cars were rented and the rental cost. If a compact car is rented for 9 days, what could be the rental cost?

Customer	Number of Days	Rental Cost
A	7	$169.00
B	10	$241.00
C	8	$193.00

Use the strategy.

Study the differences between the costs. Customer A rented a car for the least number of days and paid the least amount. Customer C rented a car for one day more than Customer A, and paid $193 − $169 or $24 more. Customer B rented a car for two days more than Customer C, and paid $241 − $193 or $48 more.

The pattern seems to be $24 more for each additional day. So a 9-day rental would probably cost $24 more than an 8-day rental.

$$\$193 + \$24 = \$217$$

The rental cost for 9 days could be $217.

Solve.

1. At a car rental agency, one customer was charged $14.40 for 60 miles. A different customer was charged $19.20 for 80 miles. How much might a customer pay for 70 miles?

2. Three car buyers got 4-year loans at the same interest rate. Person A borrowed $10,000 and pays $259 per month. Person B borrowed 11,000 and pays $284.90 per month. If Person C borrowed $12,000, how much is the monthly payment?

Answer _____

Answer _____

Solve.

3. Fred made a mistake when he copied the monthly payment amounts for a 3-year loan of $6000.

Rate	12%	13%	14%	15%
Payment	$179	$202	$205	$208

Which amount is wrong? What might the correct amount be?

Answer _____

4. A customer wants to borrow $8500 for 3 years. The payments on an $8000 loan would be $273.60. The payments on a $9000 loan would be $307.80. How much will the payments be for the loan of $8500?

Answer _____

5. A person with a driver-rating factor of 2.0 pays $240 for a certain policy. The same policy costs $300 for a person with a driver-rating factor of 2.5. How much would the same policy cost for a person with a driver-rating factor of 3.0?

Answer _____

6. Jo Ellen made a list of her gasoline purchases for one month. She paid the same price per gallon each time. Jo Ellen made a mistake on one of the prices. Which price is probably wrong? What might the correct price be?

10 gal for $13.99   14 gal for $19.60
15 gal for $29.90   11 gal for $15.39

Answer _____

7. Several cars were driven the same distance but used different amounts of gasoline, as shown in the list below. For some cars, the rate of gas usage in miles per gallon (mpg) is also listed. What are the missing numbers in the list?

Car	Gallons	mpg
A	20	50
B	25	40
C	40	25
D	100	10
E	50	_____
F	80	_____

8. Here is a list of labor costs at a repair shop, but there is a mistake in one of the amounts. Cross out the mistake and write the correct amount.

8 hours	$232.00
11.5 hours	$353.50
5 hours	$145.00
3.5 hours	$101.50

Answer _____

115

Yearly Automobile Expenses

Many people do not realize how much they spend to own and operate a car. Some of the costs, such as maintenance and gasoline, vary from month to month. Other costs, such as insurance and license plate fees, may stay the same each year.

The charts show estimates of two persons' automobile expenses. Find the yearly and monthly expenses in each category. Then add to find the total yearly and monthly expenses.

	Category	Jack's Estimated Expenses	Yearly Expenses	Monthly Expenses
1.	Depreciation (second year)	15% of $9500		
2.	Insurance	$324 twice per year		
3.	Gasoline	$15/wk × 52 weeks (average)		
4.	Maintenance	$180 twice per year		
5.	License plate fees	$65 per year		
6.	TOTAL			

	Category	Jill's Estimated Expenses	Yearly Expenses	Monthly Expenses
7.	Depreciation (first year)	30% of $12,000		
8.	Insurance	$285 twice per year		
9.	Gasoline	$24/wk × 52 weeks (average)		
10.	Maintenance	$120 twice per year		
11.	License plate fees	$75 per year		
12.	TOTAL			

13. If Jack drives 11,000 miles this year, about how much is the cost per mile? (Use the answer from Exercise 6.)

14. If Jill drives 13,000 miles this year, about how much is the cost per mile? (Use the answer from Exercise 12.)

Answer _____

Answer _____

Unit 5 Review

Solve.

1. Find the sticker price of a new car that has a base price of $8624, destination charge of $165, and these options:

   Air conditioning $597
   Rear-window defroster $89

   Answer _____

2. Maria rented a minivan for $37 per day for 8 days and drove 1452 miles. She was allowed 150 free miles per day, and was charged $0.20 for each additional mile. What was the total rental cost?

   Answer _____

3. Cory borrowed $9000 and must make payments of $303 per month for 3 years. What is the total of the monthly payments? What is the total amount of interest paid?

   Answer _____

4. The yearly base premium for Wally's automobile insurance is $197.60. If his driver-rating factor is 3.7, how much is his yearly premium?

   Answer _____

5. Rosa filled her car's gasoline tank on April 6. Find the number of miles she has driven since April 1, and the miles per gallon.

Date	Odometer	Amount
April 1	62,458	full
April 6	62,702	11.4 gal

   Answer _____

6. Suppose gasoline costs $1.55 per gallon. If your car gets 30 miles per gallon, find the cost of gasoline for a 900-mile trip.

   Answer _____

7. A car was purchased for $12,300. Its value depreciated 65% in the first four years. Find the approximate trade-in value after four years.

   Answer _____

8. Kyle had his car's air conditioning serviced. The repair shop replaced 4 pounds of refrigerant and charged $3.65 per pound. The labor charge was $22.85. What was the total charge?

   Answer _____

9. Laura can buy a monthly train pass for $68 or single-ride tickets for $2.30. She rides the train to and from work 16 days per month. How much money would she save each month by buying a monthly pass?

   Answer _____

10. Here are Zachary's approximate car expenses for one year. Find the total yearly expenses.

    Insurance $720
    Depreciation $1500
    License $32
    Gasoline $960
    Maintenance $500

    Answer _____

OWNING A HOME

Buying a House: Down Payment

Few people can afford to pay cash when purchasing a house. Instead, they make a cash down payment and borrow the rest of the money. The amount of the down payment is usually between 10% and 40% of the selling price of the house. The money borrowed is called a **mortgage** loan. There are some special funds set aside for qualified first-time buyers that have lower interest rates and require less of a down payment.

EXAMPLE 1   Alice and George Ramirez are buying a house for $62,500. A 15% down payment is required. What is the amount of the mortgage loan?

First, find the down payment: $0.15 \times \$62,500 = \$9375$

Selling price		Down payment		Mortgage loan
$62,500	−	$9375	=	$53,125

EXAMPLE 2   Mary Greer bought a $57,000 house and made a $9000 down payment. She must pay the balance in $576 monthly payments which include 12% interest. How much of the first month's payment is interest? How much is applied to the balance due?

The amount of the mortgage loan is $57,000 − $9000 or $48,000. Find the amount of the first month's payment that will be interest. Subtract to find the amount that will apply to the principal.

Principal		Rate		Time		Interest
$48,000	×	0.12	×	$\frac{1}{12}$	=	$480

Payment		Interest		Principal
$576	−	$480	=	$96

Complete the table to find the down payments and mortgage loans.

	Buyer	Selling Price	% Down	Down Payment	Mortgage Loan
1.	Linda Pinchfield	$80,500	20%		
2.	Joe and Sue Wong	$120,000	25%		
3.	Arnie Thompson	$90,000	15%		
4.	Ed and Tom Brown	$110,000	35%		

5. If Mary Greer had compared mortgage rates at several banks, she could have obtained a loan at 10% interest. How much would she have owed for interest the first month?
Refer to Example 2.

6. Ron Genicola heard about a special fund to help first-time buyers. He bought a house for $60,000. He could make a 5% down payment and borrow the remaining amount at 8% interest for 30 years. His monthly payment is $418. How much of the first payment is interest?

Answer _____

Answer _____

Buying a House: Closing Costs

A number of fees are included in the cost of buying a house. These fees, called **closing costs,** may include fees for the bank's lawyers, credit checks, property taxes, survey and inspection of property, and preparation of documents. Financing charges may also include **points.** One point is 1% of the loan. To find the closing costs, add all the bank fees.

1. Eleanor Phillips is getting a $40,000 bank loan. Complete the table to find her closing costs.

Fee	Amount
Credit report	$ 35
Loan origination: 2% of loan	
Abstract of title	60
Attorney fee	100
Document stamp: 0.3% of loan	
Processing fee: 1% of loan	
Points: 1% of loan	
TOTAL	

2. John Reilly is buying a $72,800 home with a $60,000 mortgage loan. Find his total closing costs.

Fee	Amount
Appraisal fee	$ 35
Credit report	25
Title search	175
Legal fees	250
Service fee: 2% of loan	
Processing fee: 1% of loan	
Points: 2% of loan	
TOTAL	

3. Jack Mendez is getting a $50,000 mortgage loan. Find his closing costs.

Fee	Amount
Credit report	$ 40
Loan origination: 2% of loan	
Attorney fee	300
Processing fee: 1% of loan	
Title and insurance	45
Points: 1.5% of loan	
TOTAL	

4. Sharon Urich is getting a $45,000 condominium with a $35,000 mortgage loan. Find her closing costs.

Fee	Amount
Credit report	$ 25
Title search	85
Service fee: 1.5% of loan	
Legal fees	150
Processing fee: 1% of loan	
Geologic survey	110
Points: 3% of loan	
TOTAL	

5. Refer to Exercise 2. John has saved $14,800. How much is John Reilly's down payment and closing costs? Does he have enough money saved?

6. Refer to Exercise 4. Sharon has saved $13,000. How much is Sharon's down payment and closing costs? Does she have enough saved?

Answer _____

Answer _____

OWNING A HOME

Mortgages: Monthly Payments

Banks charge interest when giving mortgage loans. A table such as the one at the right can be used to find monthly mortgage payments for different interest rates and time periods. Mortgage payments include interest and an amount which is applied to reduce the loan.

Monthly Payments per $1000 Loan			
Interest Rate	15-Year Loan	20-Year Loan	30-Year Loan
8%	$9.56	$8.37	$7.34
9%	$10.15	$9.00	$8.05
10%	$10.75	$9.66	$8.78
11%	$11.37	$10.33	$9.53
12%	$12.01	$11.01	$10.29
13%	$12.66	$11.72	$11.06
14%	$13.32	$12.44	$11.85
15%	$14.00	$13.17	$12.64
16%	$14.69	$13.91	$13.45

EXAMPLE   Jake Dempsey borrowed $30,000 at an interest rate of 11% for 15 years. What is his monthly mortgage payment?

The payment is $11.37 per $1000. Find the amount of the loan in thousands. Then multiply by $11.37.

$$\$30,000 \div \$1000 = 30$$

Monthly payment: $30 \times \$11.37 = \$341.10$.

Solve.

1. Joyce Rogers has a mortgage loan for $120,000 at 12% for 20 years. What is her monthly payment?

Answer _____

2. Ellen and Cindy Arnolds have a mortgage loan of $70,000 at 14% for 15 years. If they share the monthly payments equally, how much does each person pay?

Answer _____

3. Jim Winters buys a house for $130,000 and makes a down payment of $40,000. If his loan is at 15% for 30 years, what is his monthly payment?

Answer _____

4. Ann and Peter Stockton buy a condominium for $85,000 and make a down payment of $25,000. If their 20-year loan is at 10% instead of 11%, how much will they save on each monthly payment?

Answer _____

5. The terms of Cathy Sullivan's mortgage loan are 13% for 20 years. If she borrows $50,000, what is her monthly payment?

Answer _____

6. Over the 20 years, Cathy Sullivan will make 240 monthly payments. How much will she actually pay for her mortgage loan?

Answer _____

OWNING A HOME

Mortgages: Adjustable Rate

Interest rates vary from year to year. For that reason, most banks offer two kinds of mortgages. A **fixed-rate mortgage** has the same interest rate during each year of the loan. The loan agreement states the monthly payment for each month of the entire loan period.

An **adjustable-rate mortgage** usually starts with a lower interest rate than a fixed-rate mortgage. However, the interest rate and monthly payments are increased or decreased periodically. The mortgage agreement includes a limit on the amount the rate can change, such as 2% per year or 5% during the loan period.

Monthly Payments per $1000 Loan			
Interest Rate	15-Year Loan	20-Year Loan	30-Year Loan
8%	$ 9.56	$ 8.37	$ 7.34
9%	$10.15	$ 9.00	$ 8.05
10%	$10.75	$ 9.66	$ 8.78
11%	$11.37	$10.33	$ 9.53
12%	$12.01	$11.01	$10.29
13%	$12.66	$11.72	$11.06
14%	$13.32	$12.44	$11.85
15%	$14.00	$13.17	$12.64
16%	$14.69	$13.91	$13.45

Complete the table to compare the monthly payments for the first year.

	Amount of Loan	15-Year Fixed Rate	Monthly Payment	15-Year Adjustable	Monthly Payment	Monthly Difference
1.	$50,000	10%	*$537.50*	8%	*$478.00*	*$59.50*
2.	$80,000	10%		9%		
3.	$100,000	12%		11%		
4.	$70,000	15%		12%		
5.	$60,000	12%		10%		

6. George Wisneski took out a 30-year adjustable-rate mortgage loan for $40,000 at 10%. If the interest rate for a fixed-rate is 12%, how much less is George's monthly payment?

Answer _____

7. How much less does George pay for his mortgage during the first year?

Answer _____

8. At the end of the first year, the interest rate on George's mortgage went up to 11%. What was his new monthly payment? (Use $40,000 as the amount of loan.)

Answer _____

9. At the end of the second year, the interest rate on George's mortgage went up to 13%. Find how much more he pays per year for an adjustable-rate mortgage than a fixed-rate mortgage of 12%. (Use $40,000 as the amount of loan.)

Answer _____

OWNING A HOME
Using Electricity

Electrical power is measured in watts or kilowatts. A **kilowatt** is equal to 1000 watts, or the amount of electricity used by ten 100-watt light bulbs. Electrical usage is measured in **kilowatt-hours.** If you shine ten 100-watt bulbs for 1 hour, you use one kilowatt-hour of electricity.

If you know the number of watts that an appliance uses, you can estimate the electrical usage for a length of time.

EXAMPLE   Suppose a 600-watt microwave oven is used about 15 hours per month. How many kilowatt-hours does the oven use per month? If the electric company charges 8.2 cents per KWH, what is the cost of electricity for the microwave oven for a month?

Watts Kilowatts
600 ÷ 1000 = 0.6

Kilowatts Hours KWH
0.6 × 15 = 9 KWH

The microwave oven uses 9 KWH if it is used 15 hours per month. The cost is 8.2 cents × 9, or 73.8 cents per month.

Solve.

1. An electric refrigerator uses 250 watts of electricity. How many kilowatt-hours will it use in 30 days if the refrigerator runs 9 hours per day?

Answer _____

2. Suppose six 60-watt light bulbs are turned on for 3 hours each day. How many kilowatt-hours of electricity are used by those bulbs in seven days?

Answer _____

The electrical usage of appliances varies depending on size, the efficiency of the appliance, and the operating conditions. For example, a refrigerator uses more power if the door is opened frequently.

The chart at the right shows the average number of kilowatt-hours that various appliances use each month. Find the average cost of operating each appliance if the electricity costs 8 cents per KWH.

	Appliance	Usage per Month (KWH)	Monthly Cost
3.	Clock	2	
4.	Clothes dryer	83	
5.	Water heater	400	
6.	Vacuum cleaner	4	
7.	Washing machine	37	
8.	Color television	46	
9.	Range with oven	98	
10.	Stereo	109	
11.	Iron	12	
12.	Toaster	3	

OWNING A HOME

Reading Electric & Gas Meters

Most homes have electric meters with four dials like the ones shown below. These dials move to show the usage of electricity in kilowatt-hours. Usually once a month, someone from the electric company reads the meter. By subtracting the meter reading from the previous month's readings, the company can tell how much electricity you used in one month.

To read the meter, begin at the leftmost dial. Record the smaller of the two numbers that the hand on the dial is between. Do this for all the dials. The four numbers show the current reading of kilowatt-hours (KWH) used.

1428 kilowatt-hours

EXAMPLE Suppose the meter above shows a customer's reading for August 1. If the reading for July 1 was 0637, how many kilowatt-hours were used during July? If the cost of electricity is $0.07 per KWH, how much will the customer be charged?

Subtract to find the number of KWH used.   1428 − 0637 = 791
Multiply 791 by the cost per KWH.   791 × $0.07 = $55.37

Gas meters have three dials that are read in the same way as electric meters. Gas usage is measured in units of a hundred cubic feet, or CCF.

Write the meter reading in KWH's (kilowatt-hours).

1.

Answer _____

2.

Answer _____

Write the meter reading in CCF's (hundred cubic feet).

3.

Answer _____

4.

Answer _____

5. Last month Bertha's electric meter read 1574 KWH. This month it reads 1838 KWH. How many kilowatt-hours did she use during the month? How much is the bill if the cost is $0.08 per KWH?

Answer _____

6. Last month Ross Taylor's gas meter read 340 CCF. This month the reading was 496 CCF. He pays $0.52 per CCF, plus a service charge of $2.50. What was his bill?

Answer _____

Property Insurance

To get a mortgage loan from a bank, you must buy insurance for your house or property. Insurance can financially protect you or the mortgage holder from loss by fire or theft. Many people who rent also have insurance to protect their belongings.

EXAMPLE   Al Wong's basic homeowner's insurance for his house and contents costs $240 per year. This cost is called an **insurance premium.** In addition to the basic insurance, Al wants to insure a camera that costs $550. If the company charges $0.90 per $100 of value, what will Al's total insurance premium be?

Value of camera in hundreds:	$550 ÷ $100 = 5.5
Cost of insuring the camera:	5.5 × $0.90 = $4.95
Total insurance cost:	$240 + $4.95 = $244.95

Complete this table to find the annual insurance premium for each item.

	Item	Value	Rate per $100 Value	Annual Premium
1.	Gold ring	$800	$1.70	
2.	Coin collection	$700	$2.50	
3.	Electric guitar	$1200	$3.00	
4.	Stamp collection	$2000	$1.50	

---

5. Marge Wiley's homeowner's insurance has a basic premium of $340. She also wants to insure a violin worth $400. The rate for musical instruments is $2.50 per $100 of value. What is her total premium?

Answer _____

6. Paul and Shirley Hartwig want to insure a condominium for $60,000. The insurance rate is $6.00 per $1000. What will their annual premium be?

Answer _____

7. Peter Wolcott built a frame house that he wants to insure for $80,000. The rate is $6.60 per $1000. What is his premium?

Answer _____

8. If Peter puts a tile roof on his house, the insurance rate will go down to $6.50 per $1000 because tile is fireproof. How much will he save per year on insurance costs if he adds a tile roof?

Answer _____

OWNING A HOME
Rental Costs

When you rent an apartment, it is important to understand clearly what costs and responsibilities you will have in addition to your monthly rent. Renters often pay a **security deposit.** This money is held by the landlord for unexpected costs, such as damages caused by the renter. Usually a written lease explains what types of repairs you are expected to make and whether or not you must pay your own utilities.

EXAMPLE   Sue and Jill Ardant rent an apartment for $350 per month. When they sign the lease, they must pay first and last month's rent, plus a security deposit of $200. How much will they spend to rent the apartment?

First month's rent		Last month's rent		Security deposit		Total
$350	+	$350	+	$200	=	$900

Solve.

1. Sharon found an apartment for $325 per month. To rent it, she will need to pay first month's rent and a $300 security deposit. Utilities will be $90 extra. What will she spend to rent the apartment the first month?

Answer _____

2. Joe rents an apartment for $400 per month. He estimates that he will pay $50 per month for electricity and $75 per month for parking. How much will he be spending per month on rent, electricity, and parking?

Answer _____

3. Bill and Jose decided to share an apartment that costs $500 a month. They also pay $60 a month for electricity, $30 for gas, $5 for water, and $7 for garbage pickup. If they share the cost equally, how much will each person pay a month?

Answer _____

4. When Phyllis moved out of her apartment, she checked her lease and found that she needed to have the carpets cleaned in order to get back her security deposit of $400. The landlord charged her $45 for the cleaning. How much was left of the $400 after Phyllis paid for the carpet cleaning?

Answer _____

5. The average cost of heating a one-bedroom apartment in Chicago is $80 per month during the 6-month winter season. Julie wants to rent an apartment for a year. Which is less expensive, one with heat included for $450 per month, or one without heat included for $390 per month?

Answer _____

6. When Eleanor rented her new apartment, she agreed to have the living room repainted every 5 years. The painting costs $300. How much extra per month is Eleanor spending for the apartment if she stays for 5 years?

Answer _____

PROBLEM-SOLVING STRATEGY
Use a Formula

A formula shows a relationship between quantities. For example, the formula $I = p \times r \times t$ shows that interest is the product of the principal, rate, and time. Formulas can be used to solve problems.

A person who owns a home must pay real estate taxes and fire insurance for the home. Some mortgage companies require a portion of taxes and insurance to be paid along with the regular mortgage payment. The total monthly payment is often referred to by the initials PITI, for Principal, Interest, Taxes, and Insurance.

If a family is thinking of buying a home, they should talk with a mortgage lender to determine how large of a monthly mortgage payment they can afford. The maximum payment is based on gross income and debts. Some banks use a formula such as this.

MORTGAGE PAYMENT AFFORDABILITY FORMULA

Choose A or B, whichever is less:

(A) PITI = 26% × gross income

(B) PITI = (32% × gross income) − other debt payments

PITI = principal + interest + real estate taxes + fire insurance

---

Read the problem.

Rose is applying for a mortgage. Her gross income is $2800 per month and she has debt payments of $240 per month. How much can she afford for PITI each month?

Use the formula.

(A) PITI = 26% × $2800 = $728

(B) PITI = (32% × $2800) − $240
   = $896 − $240
   = $656

Solve the problem.

Choose the amount which is less, $656. So, Rose can afford $656 per month for principal, interest, taxes, and insurance.

Solve. Use the formulas shown above.

---

1. Colleen earns $2200 per month. She does not have any debts. How much can she afford to spend each month for PITI?

2. Travis earns $2400 per month. He has a car payment of $190 per month and no other debts. How much can he afford for housing payments (PITI)?

Answer _____

Answer _____

Solve.

3. Olivia earns $3700 per month. She has a car payment of $250 and other debt payments of $120. How much can she afford to spend each month for PITI? Use the formula on page 126.

Answer _____

4. Mr. Ogawa earns $2600 per month. Mrs. Ogawa works part-time and earns $1500 per month. They have monthly debt payments of $230. How much can they afford to spend each month for PITI?

Answer _____

5. Most people can afford a house that costs about twice their yearly income. About what income is needed to buy a house for $88,000?

Answer _____

6. If a family has gross income of $52,000, about how much can they afford to pay for a house?

Answer _____

7. The interest formula $I = p \times r \times t$, may also be expressed as $p = \dfrac{I}{r \times t}$. Find the principal if the rate is 9% and the interest for one year is $5040.

Answer _____

8. The interest formula, $I = p \times r \times t$, may also be expressed as $t = \dfrac{I}{p \times r}$. Find the time if the rate is 10%, the principal is $35,000, and the interest is $1750.

Answer _____

9. Frederick Reese is getting a mortgage. The payment for principal and interest each month will be $755. The real estate taxes are $1070 per year. The fire insurance is $250 per year. One-twelfth of the taxes and insurance will be added to Frederick's payment each month. How much will Frederick pay for PITI each month?

Answer _____

10. Amanda Dixon is getting a mortgage. The payment for principal and interest each month will be $808. The real estate taxes are $1288 per year. The fire insurance is $260 per year. One-twelfth of the taxes and insurance will be added to Amanda's payment each month. How much will she pay for PITI each month?

Answer _____

OWNING A HOME
Using Area and Perimeter Formulas

EXAMPLE 1 What is the area of the front face of this brick?

The area of a rectangle is the length times the width.

$$A = l \times w$$
$$A = 19.5 \times 5.5$$
$$A = 107.25 \text{ square centimeters (cm}^2)$$

What is the perimeter of the front face of the brick?

The perimeter is the sum of the lengths of the sides.

$$P = l + w + l + w \text{ or } 2l + 2w$$
$$P = 2(19.5) + 2(5.5)$$
$$P = 50 \text{ centimeters}$$

EXAMPLE 2 What is the area of one triangular face of this roof?

The area of a triangle is $\frac{1}{2}$ times the base times the height.

$$A = \frac{1}{2} \times b \times h$$
$$A = \frac{1}{2} \times 27 \times 14.8$$
$$A = 199.8 \text{ square feet (sq ft or ft}^2)$$

What is the perimeter of the triangle above? The other two sides are 20 feet each.

$$P = s + s + s$$
$$P = 20 + 20 + 27$$
$$P = 67 \text{ feet}$$

Solve.

1. Andrew Willis has a garden 8 meters long and 6 meters wide. If a gate is 0.5 meter wide, how many meters of fence will he need to enclose the garden?

Answer _____

2. Mary Mathews wishes to put a strip of trim, called molding, around the bottom and the top of her living room walls. The room is 16 feet by 14 feet. How many feet of molding are needed?

Answer _____

3. Kevin Sullivan wished to have his yard sodded. The yard is 60 ft by 40 ft. Estimate how many square feet of sod he needs.

Answer _____

4. Andrea bought some broadloom carpeting. She bought a piece measuring 9 feet by 15 feet. How many square feet did she buy?

Answer _____

Solve.

5. Find the cost of laying a concrete walk 50 feet long and 4 feet wide. The concrete costs $1.75 per square foot.

Answer _____

6. A highway cut off a corner of Jean Marino's property. The piece cut off formed a triangle whose base was 25 meters and whose height was 30 meters. How many square meters were in the triangle?

Answer _____

7. Nina Hatfield wants to build a fence all the way around a field. The field is 100 meters long and 80 meters wide. How many meters of fence will she need if she allows two meters for the gate?

Answer _____

8. A baseboard is a strip of trim along the bottom of a wall. How many feet of baseboard will be needed for a playroom measuring 28 feet by 22 feet if you allow 6 feet for the door openings?

Answer _____

9. Brenda Hill wants to buy carpeting for a room which measures 18 feet by 14 feet. Estimate how many square yards of carpet she will need.

Answer _____

10. How much will Brenda Hill have to pay for the carpet at $10 per square yard. (Refer to your answer to Exercise 9.)

Answer _____

11. A dining room floor is 40 feet wide and 90 feet long. Estimate how much it will cost to have the floor sanded at $1.25 a square yard. (There are 9 square feet in a square yard.)

Answer _____

12. A rug that measures 9 ft by 12 ft sells for $144. How much does it cost per square yard?

Answer _____

13. Ben Hendrickson is building a triangular patio. The sides measure 12 feet, 16 feet, and 20 feet. What is the perimeter of the patio?

Answer _____

14. During a 10%-off sale, Becky Schmidt bought enough carpet to cover an area 18 ft by 12 ft. The carpet regularly sold for $20 per square yard. Estimate how much Becky paid for the carpet.

Answer _____

OWNING A HOME
Volume and Surface Area

The volume of the concrete block is the number of cubic units that take up the same amount of space. The concrete block is 26 cm long, 10 cm wide, and 11 cm high.

EXAMPLE 1   What is the volume of the block?

Length		Width		Height		Volume
26	×	10	×	11	=	2860

The volume is 2860 cubic centimeters (cm^3).

EXAMPLE 2   What is the surface area of the block?

Surface area = sum of areas of surfaces

Front and back: $26 \times 11 = 286$ cm^2 each
Sides: $10 \times 11 = 110$ cm^2 each
Top and bottom: $10 \times 26 = 260$ cm^2 each

Add. $286 + 286 + 110 + 110 + 260 + 260 = 1312$

The surface area of the block is 1312 cm^2.

Solve.

1. For the basement of a house, a hole 30 ft wide, 40 ft long, and 10 ft deep was made. How many cubic feet of dirt were removed?

   Answer _____

2. A shelf will be covered with veneer on all 6 sides. The shelf is 48 inches long, 12 inches wide, and 1 inch thick. What is the surface area of the shelf?

   Answer _____

3. Terese Harper laid fresh topsoil 4 inches deep on her garden. The garden is 60 ft by 54 ft. How many cubic feet of soil did she need? (First change 4 inches to a fraction of a foot.)

   Answer _____

4. For a basement, dirt must be removed from a space that is 24 ft by 21 ft by 12 ft. Allowing 4 cubic yards to a load, how many loads of dirt must be removed? (First change the three dimensions to yards.)

   Answer _____

5. A garden shop sells firewood by the cord, which is 128 cubic feet. How many cords of wood are there in a stack which measures 12 ft by 18 ft by 6 ft?

   Answer _____

6. George Baker has a house that is about 30 ft wide, 100 ft in length, and 40 ft in height to the beginning of the roof. To estimate the amount of paint he needs, find the area in square feet of the four sides of the house.

   Answer _____

Calculator Applications

Measurements are not exact. For example, suppose the length of a rectangle is measured as 17.4 cm and the width is measured as 3.8 cm. These measurements are accurate to tenths of centimeters, but the actual length and width may be a little shorter or longer. The actual length could be between 17.35 cm and 17.45 cm. The actual width may be between 3.75 and 3.85 cm.

If you multiply 17.4 by 3.8 to find the area of the rectangle, not all of the digits in the product will be accurate. Compare the results at the right. Notice that the actual area may vary from 65.06 to 67.18. Because the digits of 66.12 are not all accurate, it makes more sense to report the product as 66 cm² instead of 66.12 cm².

Length		Width		Area
17.35	⊗	3.75	⊜	65.0625
17.4	⊗	3.8	⊜	66.12
17.45	⊗	3.85	⊜	67.1825

Here is an easy way to decide how to round the product when finding area. Look at the factors to see which one has fewer **significant digits**. Significant digits are the nonzero digits, plus zeros that are between nonzero digits. A measurement is less *accurate* if it has fewer significant digits. When you multiply measurements, the product should be rounded to the same number of significant digits as the less accurate factor.

EXAMPLE   Find the area of a rectangle that measures 60.2 m by 137.5 m.

60.2 ⊗ 137.5 ⊜ 8277.5

3 significant digits   4 significant digits

If you round 8277.5 to 3 significant digits, the result is 8280. So the area of the rectangle should be reported as 8280 m².

Write the number of significant digits in each number.

1. 25 _____   2. 47.1 _____   3. 10.7 _____   4. 40 _____

5. 0.7 _____   6. 9.408 _____   7. 2300 _____   8. 0.09 _____

The dimensions of a rectangle are given. Use a calculator to find the area. Round the product so it has the same number of significant digits as the less accurate factor.

9. 7.5 m × 8.2 m _____   10. 0.8 m × 0.9 m _____

11. 16.5 ft × 203 ft _____   12. 47 in. × 30.5 in. _____

13. 62 cm × 0.6 cm _____   14. 132.8 mi × 50.7 mi _____

Insulation and Roofing

Houses are built with **insulation** in the walls to prevent heat loss. Insulation for some buildings may be soft, flexible blankets made of fiberglass. The insulation comes in several widths so that it fits exactly between the boards in a wall or ceiling.

EXAMPLE 1 Estimate the cost of insulating the ceiling of a house that is 30 ft wide and 50 ft long. One package of insulating material covers 48 square feet and costs $30. Estimate the number of packages needed by using the formula for area of a rectangle, $A = l \times w$.

Area of ceiling:	$30 \times 50 = 1500$ sq ft
Number of packages needed:	$1500 \div 48 = 31.25$ or about 32
Cost:	32 packages $\times$ $30 = $960

Solve.

---

1. Susan Winters is insulating a ceiling that is 40 ft wide and 60 ft long. The insulation costs $55 per package and each package covers 64 sq ft. Estimate how much the insulation will cost.

   Answer _____

2. Fred Drew decided to insulate one wall of his den. He chose insulation that costs $40 a package. Each package covers 48 sq ft. The wall is 3 yards by 5 yards. Estimate the insulation cost.

   Answer _____

Roofing shingles are sold by the square. A **square** of shingles covers a 100-square-foot section of the roof.

EXAMPLE 2 Estimate the cost of shingling a roof which measures 2400 square feet. The shingles cost about $40 per square and the labor charge for installation is $50 per square.

Number of squares needed:	$2400 \div 100 = 24$
Cost of shingles:	24 squares $\times$ $40 = $960
Cost of labor:	24 squares $\times$ $50 = $1200
Estimated total cost:	$960 + $1200 = $2160

Solve.

---

3. Estimate the cost of roofing a building with 3000 square feet of roof. Shingles cost $35 per square. The labor charge is $30 per square.

   Answer _____

4. Estimate the cost of roofing the building shown at the right. Shingles cost $50 per square. Labor is $30 per square.

   Answer _____

Floors and Plumbing

Tiles are used for floors in kitchens, bathrooms, and other rooms of a house. The tiles come in different materials and are sold either by the carton or individually.

EXAMPLE Estimate the cost of putting a new tile floor in the kitchen that measures 15 ft by 12 ft. One carton of tiles costs $20 and will cover 50 sq ft. However, you cannot buy part of a carton.

Area of floor: $12 \times 15 = 180$ square feet
Number of cartons: $180 \div 50 = 3.6$

You will need 4 cartons at $20 each. The cost will be about $80.

Solve.

1. Tom plans to tile a bathroom that measures 6 ft by 8 ft. One carton of tiles costs $35 and will cover 40 square feet. How much will the tiles cost?

Answer _____

3. Susan rents an apartment and wants to put a new tile floor in the bathroom. Her landlady will pay for the tiles if Susan does the work. The tiles are 6 in. by 6 in. and the floor measures 10 ft by 8 ft. How many tiles will Susan need? (First find the number of tiles along the length and width.)

Answer _____

2. The floor plan of a kitchen is shown below. Find the cost of tiling the floor. The tiles cost $30 per carton. Each carton covers 30 square feet.

Answer _____

Plumbing repairs can be expensive, and if not done properly other damages can occur. It is important to hire a plumber or plumbing company that will guarantee the work.

4. Gina Martin hired a plumber to fix four clogged drains. The basic service charge was $42 for the first hour. The cost for additional time was $9.50 per 15 minutes. If the job took $1\frac{1}{2}$ hours, what was the cost?

Answer _____

5. Joy and Mark Jacobs hired a plumber to replace a drain and install a new garbage disposal. The plumber worked $1\frac{3}{4}$ hours, and charged $98.20 for parts. What was the total cost? (Use the rates from Exercise 4.)

Answer _____

Make a Drawing

When you read a problem, you might not know at once how to solve it. When that happens, a drawing may help you decide what to do. A rough sketch is usually good enough. Make sure to label the drawing with the facts given in the problem.

Read the problem.

Tom's bedroom is 10 feet 4 inches by 14 ft 6 inches. He gets a rug that measures 9 feet by 12 feet to put in the room. If he places the rug in the center, what is the distance to the wall on each end of the rug? What is the distance to the wall on each side?

Make a drawing.

Solve the problem.

Since the rug is in the center of the room, half of the uncovered distance is at each end of the room. Subtract to find the length and width not covered. Then divide each result by 2 to find each distance from the rug to the wall.

Distance to the wall:

End: (14 ft 6 in. − 12 ft) ÷ 2   Side: (10 ft 4 in. − 9 ft) ÷ 2
    = 2 ft 6 in. ÷ 2   = 1 ft 4 in. ÷ 2
    = 1 ft 3 in.   = 16 in. ÷ 2
                                                          = 8 in.

The distance from the rug to each end of the room is 1 ft 3 in. The distance from the rug to each side of the room is 8 in.

Solve.

1. One surface of a roof is shaped like a rectangle, 20 feet wide and 16 feet high. Draw a picture of the roof surface in the space at the right.

2. The shingles and roof boards need to be replaced. How many 4-ft by 8-ft pieces of plywood would cover the roof?

Answer _____

Solve.

3. A room is 12 feet 2 inches wide and 15 feet 6 inches long. One of the longer sides of the room has two doorways each 32 inches wide. Make a drawing of the room in the space at the right.

4. How much molding is needed for the base of the four walls, not including the doorways?

Answer _____

5. The Dean's house was built on a rectangular lot that is 70 feet wide along the street. The lot is 120 feet deep. Make a drawing of the lot in the space at the right.

6. If Mr. Dean stands 12 feet from the street, how far is he from the back of the lot?

Answer _____

7. The base of the Dean's house is also shaped like a rectangle. The front of the house is 30 feet from the street and the depth of the house is 26 feet. Show this on your drawing above. What is the distance from the back of the house to the back of the lot?

Answer _____

8. The Dean's house is 44 feet wide, centered on the width of the lot. How far is it to the property line on each side?

Answer _____

9. Follow these directions to draw the patio on the Ellis's house. The drawing is started for you in the space at the right. Label the length of each side as 10 units. Then draw a line from point D in the opposite direction from C. Make the line 4 units long and label the endpoint E. Draw a straight line from E to A. The patio is the shape of polygon ABCDE.

10. What is the area of the triangle ADE?

Answer _____

11. What is the area of square ABCD? If each unit is a foot, what is the total area of the patio?

Answer _____

135

OWNING A HOME

Building a Home

There are many costs associated with building a home. Some people hire an **architect** to design the home and draw construction plans. Also, most people hire a **contractor** to construct the house. Other costs are buying the lot, paying for utility service to the lot, and landscaping.

EXAMPLE Mr. Yazzie paid $1.70 per square foot for a lot that measured 60 feet by 130 feet. How much did he pay for the lot?

Total number of square feet: $60 \times 130 = 7800$ sq ft
Total cost: $7800 \times \$1.70 = \$13,260.$

Mr. Yazzie paid $13,260 for the lot.

Solve.

1. Mr. Yazzie decided to build a five-room, one-bath house on the lot. There will be two bedrooms, each 14 ft by 12 ft, a living room 18 ft by 20 ft, a dining room 12 ft by 15 ft, a kitchen 9 ft by 12 ft, and a bathroom 7 ft by 10 ft. Complete the chart at the right to find the total number of square feet in the house.

Room	Dimensions	Area
Bedroom	14 ft × 12 ft	
Bedroom		
Living room		
Dining room		
Kitchen		
Bathroom		
TOTAL		

2. The contractor said she could build the house for $70 per square foot of floor surface. What would the construction cost be? (Use total area from the chart.)

Answer _____

3. The architect who drew the plans and supervised the construction charged a fee of 5% of the construction cost. How much was the fee?

Answer _____

4. Mr. Yazzie wants to carpet the living room and dining room. At $17.50 per square yard, estimate how much it will cost.
(Hint: 1 square yard is 9 square feet.)

Answer _____

5. The house plans show a basement that will be 24 ft wide, 30 ft long, and 9 ft deep. At $10 per cubic yard, what will be the cost to dig space for the basement?

Answer _____

6. At 80 cents per square foot tile, what will be the cost of tile for the kitchen floor?

Answer _____

7. Linoleum for the kitchen floor would cost $5.30 per square yard. How much cheaper would this be than the tile?

Answer _____

136

Buying for the Home

When you move to a new home, you might need to buy new furniture and appliances. If you are a careful shopper, you can often find bargains that will save you money.

Solve.

1. When she moved into her new home, Janet bought new furniture which would have cost $1350. By paying cash, she was given a 5% discount. How much did she save?

Answer _____

2. Edward found a store that was going out of business. He bought a television set originally priced at $425 at 25% off. How much did he save?

Answer _____

3. Alex Cortex bought a new refrigerator. The usual price of it was $895. By paying cash he saved 10%. How much was saved?

Answer _____

4. Tony Jefferson bought a refrigerator during a 20%-off sale. The refrigerator regularly sold for $575. How much did he pay?

Answer _____

5. By paying cash Paula Ling was able to buy a $450 stove for $400.50. What percent did she save?

Answer _____

6. Shana wants to buy a new air conditioner which sells for $550. If she waits until winter, she can buy it at a 20% discount. How much would it cost in the winter?

Answer _____

7. Jerry bought a stove for $600. He paid $200 down and the balance, including interest, in 12 monthly installments of $40. How much did the stove cost, including interest?

Answer _____

8. Carla Robins bought a $450 freezer and paid $50 down. The balance was to be paid in 6 monthly payments of $70.50 each. How much interest did she pay in all?

Answer _____

Comparing Costs

When you purchase building supplies or appliances, price is not the only aspect to consider. Some items may have a longer warranty than others, or require less upkeep. The energy usage of appliances should also be considered.

EXAMPLE   Marla is choosing paint for her living room. Brand A has a 10-year warranty and costs $12.99 per gallon. Brand B has a 5-year warranty and costs $8.99 per gallon. She decides to buy 2 gallons of paint. If 7% sales tax is added, what is the total cost for each brand? Which paint is the better buy?

	Brand A	Brand B
Cost for 2 gallons:	2 × $12.99 = $25.98	2 × $8.99 = $17.98
Sales tax:	$25.98 × 0.07 = $ 1.82	$17.98 × 0.07 = $ 1.26
Total:	$27.80	$19.24

Brand B costs less but might not last as long.

Solve.

1. Bonita spends about $1200 every five years to have her house painted. She got an estimate for $4500 to have vinyl siding put on the house. The siding has a 20-year warranty and will not need to be painted. She is planning to live in the house for at least 20 more years. How much money will she save by buying siding?

Answer _____

2. Richard Colson is comparing the cost of two brands of lawn fertilizer. Both are sold in 50-pound bags. Brand A costs $15 and covers 1250 sq ft. Brand B costs $13.50 and covers 675 sq ft. Which is the better buy? How much less does it cost per square foot?

Answer _____

3. Julie Kelso compares two refrigerators. Brand A cost $425 and has an estimated electrical use cost of $120 a year. Brand B costs $550 and has an estimated electrical use cost of $75 a year. If she plans to use the appliance for several years, which one is the better buy?

Answer _____

4. Peter Mangini compares two window air conditioners. Brand A has an Electrical Efficiency Rating (EER) of 8 and costs $365. Brand B has an EER of 12 and costs $550. Estimated yearly operating costs are $240 for Brand A and $160 for Brand B. If Peter plans to use the air conditioner for several years, which one is the better buy?

Answer _____

Unit 6 Review

Solve.

1. Susan Rubin bought a house for $130,000. She paid 25% down and took out a mortgage loan for the remaining money. How much was her loan?

Answer _____

2. Dick Hartman buys a condominium for $90,000 and makes a down payment of $30,000. His mortgage loan is for 20 years at 14%. The mortgage payment is $12.44 per thousand of the loan amount. What is his monthly payment?

Answer _____

3. Last month Ralph's electric meter read 2365 kilowatt-hours. This month it reads 3214 kilowatt-hours. At 7¢ per kilowatt-hour, what will Ralph's electric bill be for the month?

Answer _____

4. June and Bill Fredricks want to buy $80,000 worth of insurance for their new house. If the rate is $7.00 per $1000 of value, what will their insurance premium be?

Answer _____

5. Melissa Walker found an apartment for $530 per month. To rent it, she will need to pay first and last month's rent, plus a security deposit of $350. What will she spend to rent the apartment?

Answer _____

6. Mike Rojas put in a sidewalk 5 feet by 40 feet. If it cost him $2.50 per square foot, how much did he pay for the sidewalk?

Answer _____

7. Workers dug a hole for the basement of Sharon Anthony's house. The hole was 40 feet wide, 50 feet long, and 9 feet deep. How many cubic feet of dirt were removed from the hole?

Answer _____

8. Estimate the cost of roofing a building if the roof area is 3600 square feet. The shingles will cost $40 per square and the labor charge is $35 per square. (One square of shingles covers 100 square feet.)

Answer _____

9. Lynnette needed to hire a plumber to install a new sink. The plumber charged for 2 hours and 45 minutes of labor. The rate was $40 for the first hour and $8 for each additional 15 minutes. How much did Lynnette pay for the labor charge?

Answer _____

10. By paying cash instead of charging, Carolyn Suni bought a $350 television for $315. What percent did she save?

Answer _____

Federal Income Withholding Tax

If you are employed, your employer is probably required to withhold money from each paycheck for federal income tax. The amount of tax withheld depends on your salary, the length of the pay period (weekly, monthly, etc.) whether you are single or married, and the number of withholding allowances you claim. Withholding allowances usually include yourself, your spouse (if married), and your dependent children.

When you begin a new job, the employer will ask you to fill out a Form W-4 like the one below. With that information, your employer will use a table like the partial table at the right to compute how much to withhold from your paycheck.

SINGLE Persons—WEEKLY Payroll Period

And the wages are—		And the number of withholding allowances claimed is—				
At least	But less than	0	1	2	3	4
		The amount of income tax to be withheld shall be—				
240	250	34	28	22	16	11
250	260	35	29	24	18	12
260	270	37	31	25	19	14
270	280	38	32	27	21	15
280	290	40	34	28	22	17
290	300	41	35	30	24	18
300	310	43	37	31	25	20
310	320	44	38	33	27	21
320	330	46	40	34	28	23
330	340	47	41	36	30	24
340	350	49	43	37	31	26
350	360	50	44	39	33	27
360	370	52	46	40	34	29
370	380	53	47	42	36	30
380	390	56	49	43	37	32
390	400	58	50	45	39	33
400	410	61	52	46	40	35
410	420	64	53	48	42	36
420	430	67	56	49	43	38
430	440	70	59	51	45	39
440	450	72	62	52	46	41
450	460	75	64	54	48	42
460	470	78	67	56	49	44
470	480	81	70	59	51	45
480	490	84	73	62	52	47

------------- Cut here and give the certificate to your employer. Keep the top portion for your records. -------------

Form W-4
Department of the Treasury
Internal Revenue Service

Employee's Withholding Allowance Certificate
▶ For Privacy Act and Paperwork Reduction Act Notice, see reverse.

OMB No. 1545-0010
19

1 Type or print your first name and middle initial — Last name
RUSSELL BRADY

2 Your social security number
328-01-4346

Home address (number and street or rural route)
1245 HOME AVE

City or town, state, and ZIP code
BERWYN, IL 60402

3 Marital Status
☐ Single ☐ Married
☐ Married, but withhold at higher Single rate.
Note: If married, but legally separated, or spouse is a nonresident alien, check the Single box.

4 Total number of allowances you are claiming (from line G above or from the Worksheets on back if they apply) . . . | **4**

5 Additional amount, if any, you want deducted from each pay . . . . | **5** $

6 I claim exemption from withholding and I certify that I meet ALL of the following conditions for exemption:
• Last year I had a right to a refund of ALL Federal income tax withheld because I had NO tax liability; AND
• This year I expect a refund of ALL Federal income tax withheld because I expect to have NO tax liability; AND
• This year if my income exceeds $500 and includes nonwage income, another person cannot claim me as a dependent.
If you meet all of the above conditions, enter the year effective and "EXEMPT" here . . . . . ▶ | **6** 19

7 Are you a full-time student? (**Note:** Full-time students are not automatically exempt.) . . . . | **7** ☐Yes ☐No

Under penalties of perjury, I certify that I am entitled to the number of withholding allowances claimed on this certificate or entitled to claim exempt status.

Employee's signature ▶ *Russell Brady*   Date ▶ 5-31 , 19—

8 Employer's name and address (**Employer:** Complete 8 and 10 only if sending to IRS)

9 Office code (optional)

10 Employer identification number

EXAMPLE Russell Brady filled out the form to show that he is single and is claiming 1 withholding allowance (box 3). (If Russell had wanted to have an additional amount withheld each week, he could have written the amount on Line 5.) Russell Brady's salary is $274 per week. How much money is withheld from Russell's salary each week for federal income taxes?

In the table, 274 is between 270 and 280. Read across the row to the column labeled 1 for one withholding allowance. The amount withheld is $32.

For each exercise, the number of allowances and weekly salary of a single person are listed. Use the partial table on page 140 to find the amount withheld from each paycheck.

1. 2 allowances, $314 _____

3. 1 allowance, $289 _____

2. 0 allowances, $405 _____

4. 3 allowances, $347 _____

For each exercise, the number of allowances and weekly salary of a married person are listed. Use the partial table below to find the amount withheld from each paycheck.

5. 3 allowances, $325 _____

7. 4 allowances, $505 _____

9. 0 allowances, $401 _____

6. 2 allowances, $483 _____

8. 1 allowance, $232 _____

10. 2 allowances, $308 _____

11. Jan is married and claims 2 allowances. She earns $181 per week, and $7 is withheld from each paycheck. Suppose Jan gets a new job and earns exactly twice as much as before. How much would be withheld? Is the withholding amount twice as much as before?

Answer _____

12. Suppose Jan would like to have $560 more deducted during one year. About how much should be deducted from each of her 52 paychecks?

Answer _____

13. Rita and Jack are married. Rita earns $423 per week and claims 3 allowances. Jack works parttime, earns $156 per week, and claims 0 allowances. What is the total withheld for the couple each week? (Find each withholding amount separately.)

Answer _____

14. Refer to Exercise 13. Suppose Rita and Jack provide new W-4 Forms. Rita claims 0 allowances and Jack claims 3. How much more or less federal tax will be withheld for the couple each week?

Answer _____

MARRIED Persons–WEEKLY Payroll Period

And the wages are–		And the number of withholding allowances claimed is–				
At least	But less than	0	1	2	3	4
		The amount of income tax to be withheld shall be–				
220	230	25	19	13	7	1
230	240	26	20	14	9	3
240	250	28	22	16	10	4
250	260	29	23	17	12	6
260	270	31	25	19	13	7
270	280	32	26	20	15	9
280	290	34	28	22	16	10
290	300	35	29	23	18	12
300	310	37	31	25	19	13
310	320	38	32	26	21	15
320	330	40	34	28	22	16
330	340	41	35	29	24	18
340	350	43	37	31	25	19
350	360	44	38	32	27	21
360	370	46	40	34	28	22
370	380	47	41	35	30	24
380	390	49	43	37	31	26
390	400	50	44	38	33	27
400	410	52	46	40	34	28
410	420	53	47	41	36	30
420	430	55	49	43	37	31
430	440	56	50	44	39	33
440	450	58	52	46	40	34
450	460	59	53	47	42	36
460	470	61	55	49	43	37
470	480	62	56	50	45	39
480	490	64	58	52	46	40
490	500	65	59	53	48	42
500	510	67	61	55	49	43
510	520	68	62	56	51	45
520	530	70	64	58	52	46
530	540	71	65	59	54	48
540	550	73	67	61	55	49
550	560	74	68	62	57	51
560	570	76	70	64	58	52
570	580	77	71	65	60	54
580	590	79	73	67	61	55
590	600	80	74	68	63	57
600	610	82	76	70	64	58
610	620	83	77	71	66	60

Social Security Tax

The Federal Insurance Contributions Act (FICA) requires employers to withhold a portion of the pay of most employees for **social security** taxes. In 1990, the rate was 7.65%. The employer must contribute an amount that equals the employee's contribution and send both amounts to the federal government. The money is used to pay retirement benefits, disability benefits, medical-cost benefits, and survivor's benefits to qualified persons.

EXAMPLE   Natalie earns $429.45 per week. Using a rate of 7.65%, how much social security tax is withheld from each week's paycheck?

$$7.65\% \text{ of } \$429.45 = 0.0765 \times \$429.45$$
$$= \$32.852925$$
$$= \$32.86 \qquad \text{Round up to the next cent.}$$

People who are self-employed must pay 13.3% of their profit for social security taxes. The rate is higher because a self-employed person's contribution is not being matched by an employer's contribution. A self-employed person is required to send these taxes directly to the government in quarterly payments (every three months), along with federal income tax payments.

Find the amount of social security tax withheld for the given gross weekly pay. Use a tax rate of 7.65%.

1. $514.56

2. $202.83

3. $347.58

4. $798.45

_____   _____   _____   _____

---

5. Sue's salary is $33,000 per year. How much is withheld each year for social security tax?

Answer _____

6. Larry earns $42,750 per year. What is the total of Larry's social security contribution and his employer's matching contribution?

Answer _____

---

7. Greg is self-employed and made a profit of $37,341 in one year. How much social security tax did he owe for the year? Use a rate of 13.3%.

Answer _____

8. Louisa is self-employed and expects a profit of $12,500 in the first quarter of the year. How much social security tax should she pay for the quarter? Use a rate of 13.3%.

Answer _____

Income Reports

In January of each year, your employer will send you a Wage and Tax Statement Form, called a **Form W-2.** The W-2 form tells you how much you earned the previous year and how much was withheld for federal, state, and local income tax. It also shows the amount withheld for social security (FICA).

Form 1099 is a similar form that is used to report miscellaneous income. If your bank account earned interest, your bank sends you a Form 1099 showing how much interest was earned. If you are self-employed and companies paid you for services, the companies will send 1099 forms showing the total paid to you during the year.

OMB No. 1545-0008	
1 Control number 50040N	4 Employer's State number
	FORM W-2 **1988** Wage and Tax Statement Copy D for employer Department of the Treasury Internal Revenue Service
2 Employer's name, address, and ZIP code Merchant's Inc. 2345 State Street New York, NY 10017	3 Employer's identification number
8 Employee's social security number 222-00-3333	9 Federal income tax withheld $4,872
10 Wages, tips, other compensation $873	11 Social security tax withheld
12 Employee's name Marcia Murray 1234 Pleasant Ave. Anytown, USA Employee's address and ZIP code	
17 State income tax $3,135	

EXAMPLE The W-2 form above shows Marcia Murray's wages for a year. She also received a 1099 form from the bank that showed interest earnings of $359. What was Marcia's gross income?

Salary $32,150 + Interest income $359 = Gross income $32,509

Find the total of wages and interest income for each person.

	Name	Wages from W-2	Interest from 1099	Total
1.	P. Baty	$24,901	$389	
2.	C. Thomas	$12,073	$67	
3.	W. Myers	$34,289	$297	
4.	M. Anders	$50,388	$784	

5. Sam Snider's W-2 form showed that $834 was withheld for state tax and $490 was withheld for local tax. How much was withheld for state and local tax?

Answer _____

6. A W-2 form shows that a person received wages of $24,952. If $998.08 was withheld for state taxes, what percent of wages were withheld for state taxes?

Answer _____

Form 1040EZ

By law, most people who earn money must prepare an income tax form by April 15 of each year and send it to the Internal Revenue Service, or IRS. Each tax form includes instructions for computing **taxable income.** Tables are included for figuring the **tax liability** based on taxable income and filing status. The **filing status** can be single, married filing separately, married filing jointly, or head of household.

Some of the tax liability is already paid by withholding tax, indicated on the W-2 form. If the tax liability is greater than the amount withheld, the taxpayer owes the IRS an amount called the **balance due.** If the tax liability is less than the amount withheld, the IRS will return the extra money as a **tax refund.** All amounts on tax forms can be rounded to the nearest dollar.

New tax forms are distributed each year by the IRS. There are several different forms available. The page at the right shows a sample of **Form 1040EZ,** the easiest form to use. This form is designed for single persons with no dependents, who earned less than $50,000 income and less than $400 in interest and dividends.

Linn Wong is single and has no dependents. She can use a 1040EZ Form as shown on the page at the right. Use information from the section of her W-2 form shown and the 1040EZ to complete the exercises below.

1. Write Linn's name, address, and social security number in the spaces provided at the top of Form 1040EZ.

2. Linn's total wages are shown in Box 10 of her W-2 form. She also earned $148 interest on her savings account. Write these amounts on lines 1 and 2 of the 1040EZ. Then add and write the total on line 3. This is Linn's **adjusted gross income.**

3. Since Linn is not claimed as a dependent of someone else, check the box marked "No" and write 3,000 for her **standard deduction** on line 4. Subtract. Then write 2,000 for a **personal exemption** on line 6. Subtract. The remaining income is her **taxable income,** line 7.

4. Box 9 of Linn's W-2 form shows how much tax was withheld. Write this amount on line 8. Linn looked up her tax liability in the tax tables. It is $3287. Write this amount on line 9. Since line 8 is larger than line 9, subtract to find her refund.

5. Suppose Linn's employer had withheld $2,960 in federal tax. Would Linn get a refund (line 10) or owe (line 11)? How much?

Answer _____

To complete the tax return, Linn would sign her name, write the date, and attach a copy of her W-2 form. If she owed money she would also attach a check or money order. Then she would make a copy of the completed form 1040EZ for her records and send the original to the address provided.

Department of the Treasury - Internal Revenue Service

Form
1040EZ

Income Tax Return for
Single filers with no dependents   19—

OMB No. 1545-0675

Name & address

Use the IRS mailing label. If you don't have one, please print.

Please print your numbers like this:

0 1 2 3 4 5 6 7 8 9

L A B E L   H E R E

Print your name above (first, initial, last)

Present home address (number, street, and apt. no.). (If you have a P.O. box, see back.)

City, town, or post office, state, and ZIP code

Your social security number

Please read the instructions on the back of this form. Also, see page 13 of the booklet for a helpful checklist.

Presidential Election Campaign Fund
Do you want $1 to go to this fund?

Note: *Checking "Yes" will not change your tax or reduce your refund.* ▶

Yes No

Dollars   **Cents**

Report your income

Attach Copy B of Form(s) W-2 here

1 Total wages, salaries, and tips. This should be shown in Box 10 of your W-2 form(s). (Attach your W-2 form(s).) **1**

2 Taxable interest income of $400 or less. If the total is more than $400, you cannot use Form 1040EZ. **2**

3 Add line 1 and line 2. This is your **adjusted gross income.** **3**

Note: You must check Yes or No.

4 Can your parents or someone else claim you on their return?

☐ **Yes.** Do worksheet on back; enter amount from line E **here.**

☐ **No.** Enter 3,000 as your standard deduction. **4**

5 Subtract line 4 from line 3. If line 4 is larger than line 3, enter 0. **5**

6 If you checked the "Yes" box on line 4, enter **0.**
If you checked the "No" box on line 4, enter **1,950.**
This is your **personal exemption.** **6**

7 Subtract line 6 from line 5. If line 6 is larger than line 5, enter 0. This is your **taxable income.** **7**

Figure your tax

8 Enter your Federal income tax withheld from Box 9 of your W-2 form(s). **8**

9 Use the **single** column in the tax table on pages 37–42 of the Form 1040A/1040EZ booklet to find the **tax** on the amount shown on **line 7** above. Enter the amount of tax. **9**

Refund or amount you owe

Attach tax payment here

10 If line 8 is larger than line 9, subtract line 9 from line 8. Enter the **amount of your refund.** **10**

11 If line 9 is larger than line 8, subtract line 8 from line 9. Enter the **amount you owe.** Attach check or money order for the full amount, payable to "Internal Revenue Service." **11**

Sign your return

I have read this return. Under penalties of perjury, I declare that to the best of my knowledge and belief, the return is true, correct, and complete.

Your signature   Date

For IRS Use Only—Please do not write in boxes below.

PAYING TAXES

Practice with Form 1040EZ

Suppose you are single and your parents or someone else *can* claim you on their return. If you had interest income, you must file a return if your total income was $500 or more. If you did *not* have interest income, you must file a return if your total wages were $3000 or more. You *cannot* take a personal exemption. (See line 6 of 1040EZ.)

On line 4 of Form 1040EZ, you can deduct from $500 to $3000 of your income. A worksheet for finding the exact deduction is provided on the back of Form 1040EZ. If your taxable income is less than $18,000, you can estimate the amount of tax by multiplying the taxable income by 15%. The exact amount of tax would be found by using a tax table.

Complete each column of the chart. Line 10 or 11 in each column should be blank. Refer to a copy of Form 1040EZ.

	1.	2.	3.	4.	5.
NAME OF TAXPAYER	J. Sullivan	A. Rosner	B. Vincent	M. Riga	C. Sawada
Line 1 Wages	$1307	$4589	$21,760	$16,304	$465
Line 2 Interest	43	0	352	185	290
Line 3 Adj. gross income	*1350*				
Line 4 Deduction	1307	3000	3000	3000	500
Line 5 Line 3 − line 4	*43*				
Line 6 Personal exemption	0	0	2000	2000	0
Line 7 Taxable income	*43*				
Line 8 Tax withheld	0	264	2691	1582	0
Line 9 Tax (Use 15% of line 7.) Round to dollars.	*6*				
Line 10 Refund					
Line 11 Amount you owe	*$6*				

6. Lori Raymas is single and is not claimed on anyone else's tax return. She earned wages of $18,394 and earned no interest. Her employer withheld $1980 for federal tax.

Her taxable income is _____

Her tax liability (15%) is _____

The amount she owes is _____

7. Luke is single and is not claimed on anyone else's tax return. He earned $13,487 from one job and $5324 from another. The federal taxes withheld were $1279 and $572.

His taxable income is _____

His tax liability (15%) is _____

The amount he owes is _____

146

Calculator Applications

The memory keys of a calculator are helpful when a computation requires several steps. Compare these memory keys with the ones on your calculator. Are the keys labeled the same way?

M+ Adds the number in the display to the number in the memory.

M− Subtracts the number in the display from the number in the memory.

MR Recalls and displays the number that is in memory. (MR stands for *Memory Recall*.)

AC Clears the display and erases the number in memory. (AC stands for *All Clear*.) Press this key before starting a new problem.

EXAMPLE   Use a calculator to find the value of
$84.50 + (35 \times \$4.30) - \$36.85 + (24 \times \$5.47)$.

Press: Display:

84.5 **M+**   84.5

35 **×** 4.30 **=** **M+**   150.5

36.85 **M−**   36.85

24 **×** 5.47 **=** **M+**   131.28

MR   329.43

The value is $329.43.

Use a calculator with memory keys. Copy the display for each step and the total. Watch the signs carefully.

Total value

1.	$65.80	+	(7 × $9.20)	−	($60.76 ÷ 2)	+	$11.98	
	65.8		*64.4*		*30.38*		*11.98*	

2.	(2 × $5392)	+	$993	−	(16 × $430)	−	$2399	

3.	(982 ÷ 2)	−	274	+	(32 × 45)	+	(65 × 30)	

4.	(4 × 19.23)	−	(3 × 6.2)	−	2.26	+	(18.4 ÷ 5)	

5.	$458.77	+	(3 × $28.95)	+	(2 × $39.44)	+	$12.59	

Using Tax Tables

The Internal Revenue Service (IRS) provides tax tables with the instructions for federal income tax forms. Suppose you know a person's taxable income and filing status. These tables can be used to find the tax liability. By comparing the tax liability to the tax withheld, you can compute the amount owed or balance due.

EXAMPLE   Percy Jones has a taxable income of $6380. His filing status is single and $689 tax was withheld from his pay. Does he owe or get a refund? How much?

Use the table to find the tax liability. Locate the section labeled 6,000, then the row for 6,380. This income is between 6,350 and 6,400. Read across to the column marked single. The tax is $956.

Since less than $956 was withheld, he owes money. The amount owed is $956 − $689 or $267.

Use the table to find the tax liabilities for taxpayers with the following taxable incomes and filing status.

1. $12,983 Married filing jointly   _____

2. $27,045 Head of a household   _____

3. $7,502 Married filing separately   _____

4. $25,077 Single   _____

5. $23,460 Married filing jointly   _____

6. $13,298 Single   _____

7. Anne Reimer has a taxable income of $11,802. Her filing status is single and $1,893 tax was withheld from her pay.

   What is her tax liability?   _____

   Does she owe or get a refund? How much?   _____

8. Jim and Patty Barnes have a taxable income of $26,732. They are married and file a joint return. A total of $3,548 tax was withheld from their pay.

   What is their tax liability?   _____

   Do they owe or get a refund? How much?   _____

1988 Tax Table—*Continued*

If line 37 (taxable income) is—		And you are—			
At least	But less than	Single	Married filing jointly *	Married filing separately	Head of a house-hold
		Your tax is—			
5,000					
5,000	5,050	754	754	754	754
5,050	5,100	761	761	761	761
5,100	5,150	769	769	769	769
5,150	5,200	776	776	776	776
5,200	5,250	784	784	784	784
5,250	5,300	791	791	791	791
5,300	5,350	799	799	799	799
5,350	5,400	806	806	806	806
5,400	5,450	814	814	814	814
5,450	5,500	821	821	821	821
5,500	5,550	829	829	829	829
5,550	5,600	836	836	836	836
5,600	5,650	844	844	844	844
5,650	5,700	851	851	851	851
5,700	5,750	859	859	859	859
5,750	5,800	866	866	866	866
5,800	5,850	874	874	874	874
5,850	5,900	881	881	881	881
5,900	5,950	889	889	889	889
5,950	6,000	896	896	896	896
6,000					
6,000	6,050	904	904	904	904
6,050	6,100	911	911	911	911
6,100	6,150	919	919	919	919
6,150	6,200	926	926	926	926
6,200	6,250	934	934	934	934
6,250	6,300	941	941	941	941
6,300	6,350	949	949	949	949
6,350	6,400	956	956	956	956
6,400	6,450	964	964	964	964
6,450	6,500	971	971	971	971
6,500	6,550	979	979	979	979
6,550	6,600	986	986	986	986
6,600	6,650	994	994	994	994
6,650	6,700	1,001	1,001	1,001	1,001
6,700	6,750	1,009	1,009	1,009	1,009
6,750	6,800	1,016	1,016	1,016	1,016
6,800	6,850	1,024	1,024	1,024	1,024
6,850	6,900	1,031	1,031	1,031	1,031
6,900	6,950	1,039	1,039	1,039	1,039
6,950	7,000	1,046	1,046	1,046	1,046
7,000					
7,000	7,050	1,054	1,054	1,054	1,054
7,050	7,100	1,061	1,061	1,061	1,061
7,100	7,150	1,069	1,069	1,069	1,069
7,150	7,200	1,076	1,076	1,076	1,076
7,200	7,250	1,084	1,084	1,084	1,084
7,250	7,300	1,091	1,091	1,091	1,091
7,300	7,350	1,099	1,099	1,099	1,099
7,350	7,400	1,106	1,106	1,106	1,106
7,400	7,450	1,114	1,114	1,114	1,114
7,450	7,500	1,121	1,121	1,121	1,121
7,500	7,550	1,129	1,129	1,129	1,129
7,550	7,600	1,136	1,136	1,136	1,136
7,600	7,650	1,144	1,144	1,144	1,144
7,650	7,700	1,151	1,151	1,151	1,151
7,700	7,750	1,159	1,159	1,159	1,159
7,750	7,800	1,166	1,166	1,166	1,166
7,800	7,850	1,174	1,174	1,174	1,174
7,850	7,900	1,181	1,181	1,181	1,181
7,900	7,950	1,189	1,189	1,189	1,189
7,950	8,000	1,196	1,196	1,196	1,196

* This column must also be used by a qualifying widow(er).

11,000–14,000

If line 37 (taxable income) is— At least	But less than	Single	Married filing jointly *	Married filing separately	Head of a household
11,000					
11,000	11,050	1,654	1,654	1,654	1,654
11,050	11,100	1,661	1,661	1,661	1,661
11,100	11,150	1,669	1,669	1,669	1,669
11,150	11,200	1,676	1,676	1,676	1,676
11,200	11,250	1,684	1,684	1,684	1,684
11,250	11,300	1,691	1,691	1,691	1,691
11,300	11,350	1,699	1,699	1,699	1,699
11,350	11,400	1,706	1,706	1,706	1,706
11,400	11,450	1,714	1,714	1,714	1,714
11,450	11,500	1,721	1,721	1,721	1,721
11,500	11,550	1,729	1,729	1,729	1,729
11,550	11,600	1,736	1,736	1,736	1,736
11,600	11,650	1,744	1,744	1,744	1,744
11,650	11,700	1,751	1,751	1,751	1,751
11,700	11,750	1,759	1,759	1,759	1,759
11,750	11,800	1,766	1,766	1,766	1,766
11,800	11,850	1,774	1,774	1,774	1,774
11,850	11,900	1,781	1,781	1,781	1,781
11,900	11,950	1,789	1,789	1,789	1,789
11,950	12,000	1,796	1,796	1,796	1,796
12,000					
12,000	12,050	1,804	1,804	1,804	1,804
12,050	12,100	1,811	1,811	1,811	1,811
12,100	12,150	1,819	1,819	1,819	1,819
12,150	12,200	1,826	1,826	1,826	1,826
12,200	12,250	1,834	1,834	1,834	1,834
12,250	12,300	1,841	1,841	1,841	1,841
12,300	12,350	1,849	1,849	1,849	1,849
12,350	12,400	1,856	1,856	1,856	1,856
12,400	12,450	1,864	1,864	1,864	1,864
12,450	12,500	1,871	1,871	1,871	1,871
12,500	12,550	1,879	1,879	1,879	1,879
12,550	12,600	1,886	1,886	1,886	1,886
12,600	12,650	1,894	1,894	1,894	1,894
12,650	12,700	1,901	1,901	1,901	1,901
12,700	12,750	1,909	1,909	1,909	1,909
12,750	12,800	1,916	1,916	1,916	1,916
12,800	12,850	1,924	1,924	1,924	1,924
12,850	12,900	1,931	1,931	1,931	1,931
12,900	12,950	1,939	1,939	1,939	1,939
12,950	13,000	1,946	1,946	1,946	1,946
13,000					
13,000	13,050	1,954	1,954	1,954	1,954
13,050	13,100	1,961	1,961	1,961	1,961
13,100	13,150	1,969	1,969	1,969	1,969
13,150	13,200	1,976	1,976	1,976	1,976
13,200	13,250	1,984	1,984	1,984	1,984
13,250	13,300	1,991	1,991	1,991	1,991
13,300	13,350	1,999	1,999	1,999	1,999
13,350	13,400	2,006	2,006	2,006	2,006
13,400	13,450	2,014	2,014	2,014	2,014
13,450	13,500	2,021	2,021	2,021	2,021
13,500	13,550	2,029	2,029	2,029	2,029
13,550	13,600	2,036	2,036	2,036	2,036
13,600	13,650	2,044	2,044	2,044	2,044
13,650	13,700	2,051	2,051	2,051	2,051
13,700	13,750	2,059	2,059	2,059	2,059
13,750	13,800	2,066	2,066	2,066	2,066
13,800	13,850	2,074	2,074	2,074	2,074
13,850	13,900	2,081	2,081	2,081	2,081
13,900	13,950	2,089	2,089	2,089	2,089
13,950	14,000	2,096	2,096	2,096	2,096

23,000–26,000

If line 37 (taxable income) is— At least	But less than	Single	Married filing jointly *	Married filing separately	Head of a household
23,000					
23,000	23,050	4,127	3,454	4,513	3,454
23,050	23,100	4,141	3,461	4,527	3,461
23,100	23,150	4,155	3,469	4,541	3,469
23,150	23,200	4,169	3,476	4,555	3,476
23,200	23,250	4,183	3,484	4,569	3,484
23,250	23,300	4,197	3,491	4,583	3,491
23,300	23,350	4,211	3,499	4,597	3,499
23,350	23,400	4,225	3,506	4,611	3,506
23,400	23,450	4,239	3,514	4,625	3,514
23,450	23,500	4,253	3,521	4,639	3,521
23,500	23,550	4,267	3,529	4,653	3,529
23,550	23,600	4,281	3,536	4,667	3,536
23,600	23,650	4,295	3,544	4,681	3,544
23,650	23,700	4,309	3,551	4,695	3,551
23,700	23,750	4,323	3,559	4,709	3,559
23,750	23,800	4,337	3,566	4,723	3,566
23,800	23,850	4,351	3,574	4,737	3,574
23,850	23,900	4,365	3,581	4,751	3,581
23,900	23,950	4,379	3,589	4,765	3,592
23,950	24,000	4,393	3,596	4,779	3,606
24,000					
24,000	24,050	4,407	3,604	4,793	3,620
24,050	24,100	4,421	3,611	4,807	3,634
24,100	24,150	4,435	3,619	4,821	3,648
24,150	24,200	4,449	3,626	4,835	3,662
24,200	24,250	4,463	3,634	4,849	3,676
24,250	24,300	4,477	3,641	4,863	3,690
24,300	24,350	4,491	3,649	4,877	3,704
24,350	24,400	4,505	3,656	4,891	3,718
24,400	24,450	4,519	3,664	4,905	3,732
24,450	24,500	4,533	3,671	4,919	3,746
24,500	24,550	4,547	3,679	4,933	3,760
24,550	24,600	4,561	3,686	4,947	3,774
24,600	24,650	4,575	3,694	4,961	3,788
24,650	24,700	4,589	3,701	4,975	3,802
24,700	24,750	4,603	3,709	4,989	3,816
24,750	24,800	4,617	3,716	5,003	3,830
24,800	24,850	4,631	3,724	5,017	3,844
24,850	24,900	4,645	3,731	5,031	3,858
24,900	24,950	4,659	3,739	5,045	3,872
24,950	25,000	4,673	3,746	5,059	3,886
25,000					
25,000	25,050	4,687	3,754	5,073	3,900
25,050	25,100	4,701	3,761	5,087	3,914
25,100	25,150	4,715	3,769	5,101	3,928
25,150	25,200	4,729	3,776	5,115	3,942
25,200	25,250	4,743	3,784	5,129	3,956
25,250	25,300	4,757	3,791	5,143	3,970
25,300	25,350	4,771	3,799	5,157	3,984
25,350	25,400	4,785	3,806	5,171	3,998
25,400	25,450	4,799	3,814	5,185	4,012
25,450	25,500	4,813	3,821	5,199	4,026
25,500	25,550	4,827	3,829	5,213	4,040
25,550	25,600	4,841	3,836	5,227	4,054
25,600	25,650	4,855	3,844	5,241	4,068
25,650	25,700	4,869	3,851	5,255	4,082
25,700	25,750	4,883	3,859	5,269	4,096
25,750	25,800	4,897	3,866	5,283	4,110
25,800	25,850	4,911	3,874	5,297	4,124
25,850	25,900	4,925	3,881	5,311	4,138
25,900	25,950	4,939	3,889	5,325	4,152
25,950	26,000	4,953	3,896	5,339	4,166

26,000–29,000

If line 37 (taxable income) is— At least	But less than	Single	Married filing jointly *	Married filing separately	Head of a household
26,000					
26,000	26,050	4,967	3,904	5,353	4,180
26,050	26,100	4,981	3,911	5,367	4,194
26,100	26,150	4,995	3,919	5,381	4,208
26,150	26,200	5,009	3,926	5,395	4,222
26,200	26,250	5,023	3,934	5,409	4,236
26,250	26,300	5,037	3,941	5,423	4,250
26,300	26,350	5,051	3,949	5,437	4,264
26,350	26,400	5,065	3,956	5,451	4,278
26,400	26,450	5,079	3,964	5,465	4,292
26,450	26,500	5,093	3,971	5,479	4,306
26,500	26,550	5,107	3,979	5,493	4,320
26,550	26,600	5,121	3,986	5,507	4,334
26,600	26,650	5,135	3,994	5,521	4,348
26,650	26,700	5,149	4,001	5,535	4,362
26,700	26,750	5,163	4,009	5,549	4,376
26,750	26,800	5,177	4,016	5,563	4,390
26,800	26,850	5,191	4,024	5,577	4,404
26,850	26,900	5,205	4,031	5,591	4,418
26,900	26,950	5,219	4,039	5,605	4,432
26,950	27,000	5,233	4,046	5,619	4,446
27,000					
27,000	27,050	5,247	4,054	5,633	4,460
27,050	27,100	5,261	4,061	5,647	4,474
27,100	27,150	5,275	4,069	5,661	4,488
27,150	27,200	5,289	4,076	5,675	4,502
27,200	27,250	5,303	4,084	5,689	4,516
27,250	27,300	5,317	4,091	5,703	4,530
27,300	27,350	5,331	4,099	5,717	4,544
27,350	27,400	5,345	4,106	5,731	4,558
27,400	27,450	5,359	4,114	5,745	4,572
27,450	27,500	5,373	4,121	5,759	4,586
27,500	27,550	5,387	4,129	5,773	4,600
27,550	27,600	5,401	4,136	5,787	4,614
27,600	27,650	5,415	4,144	5,801	4,628
27,650	27,700	5,429	4,151	5,815	4,642
27,700	27,750	5,443	4,159	5,829	4,656
27,750	27,800	5,457	4,166	5,843	4,670
27,800	27,850	5,471	4,174	5,857	4,684
27,850	27,900	5,485	4,181	5,871	4,698
27,900	27,950	5,499	4,189	5,885	4,712
27,950	28,000	5,513	4,196	5,899	4,726
28,000					
28,000	28,050	5,527	4,204	5,913	4,740
28,050	28,100	5,541	4,211	5,927	4,754
28,100	28,150	5,555	4,219	5,941	4,768
28,150	28,200	5,569	4,226	5,955	4,782
28,200	28,250	5,583	4,234	5,969	4,796
28,250	28,300	5,597	4,241	5,983	4,810
28,300	28,350	5,611	4,249	5,997	4,824
28,350	28,400	5,625	4,256	6,011	4,838
28,400	28,450	5,639	4,264	6,025	4,852
28,450	28,500	5,653	4,271	6,039	4,866
28,500	28,550	5,667	4,279	6,053	4,880
28,550	28,600	5,681	4,286	6,067	4,894
28,600	28,650	5,695	4,294	6,081	4,908
28,650	28,700	5,709	4,301	6,095	4,922
28,700	28,750	5,723	4,309	6,109	4,936
28,750	28,800	5,737	4,316	6,123	4,950
28,800	28,850	5,751	4,324	6,137	4,964
28,850	28,900	5,765	4,331	6,151	4,978
28,900	28,950	5,779	4,339	6,165	4,992
28,950	29,000	5,793	4,346	6,179	5,006

Continued on next page

* This column must also be used by a qualifying widow(er).

Use Guess-and-Check

A good way to solve some problems is to guess the answer. Then check to see if the answer is correct, and make another guess if necessary. Your next guess will be better because you will learn from the first guess. Continue to guess and check until you find the correct answer.

Read the problem.

In one year, Mr. and Mrs. Yates had earnings of $40,600. If Mr. Yates earned $2200 more than Mrs. Yates, how much did each person earn?

Guess and check.

For Mr. Yates, start with a guess that is more than half of $40,600. Subtract to find Mrs. Yates's earnings. Then check whether the difference is $2200.

Guess 1:

Mr. Yates	$21,000
Mrs. Yates	$19,600
Difference	$ 1,400

Check:
The total earnings are $40,600 but the difference is less than $2200.

Guess 2:

Mr. Yates	$21,500
Mrs. Yates	$19,100
Difference	$ 2,400

Check:
The total earnings are $40,600 but the difference is more than $2200.

Guess 3:

Mr. Yates	$21,400
Mrs. Yates	$19,200
Difference	$ 2,200

Check:
Both the total earnings and the difference are correct.

So, Mr. Yates earned $21,400 and Mrs. Yates earned $19,200.

Solve. Use the guess-and-check strategy.

1. Linda received interest income of $375 from two accounts. One account earned $35 more than the other. How much interest income did Linda receive from each account?

2. Jason earned a total of $15,900 from two part-time jobs. If he earned $3700 more from one job than the other, how much did he earn from each job?

Answer _____

Answer _____

Solve. Use the guess-and-check strategy.

3. Mr. and Mrs. King earned a total of $50,700. Mrs. King earned twice as much as Mr. King. How much did each person earn?

Answer _____

4. Mr. and Mrs. Rosenbaum received interest income of $924 from two accounts. One account earned 3 times as much as the other. How much interest income did they receive from each account?

Answer _____

5. On one of Nellie's paychecks, $85 was withheld for state and federal taxes. The amount withheld for federal tax was $53 more than the amount withheld for state tax. How much was withheld for federal tax?

Answer _____

6. A total of $140 was deducted from Wally's paycheck for taxes and insurance. The deduction for insurance was $10 less than the deduction for taxes. How much was deducted for insurance?

Answer _____

7. In three weeks, a total of $191 was withheld from Teresa's paycheck for federal tax. The same amount was withheld for Weeks 1 and 2. The amount withheld for Week 3 was $5 more. How much was withheld in Week 3?

Answer _____

8. Brent earned $35 for three baby-sitting jobs. He earned $5 more from Job A than from Job B. He earned half as much from Job C as he did from Job B. How much did he earn from each job?

Answer _____

Form 1040A: Adjusted Gross Income

Forms 1040A can be used by single or married persons with or without dependents. A person who does not itemize or does not need to file special forms can use 1040A. The first page of Form 1040A is shown on the page at the right.

In Step 1 taxpayers must write or attach a label with their name, address, and social security number. Each taxpayer checks a box to indicate whether $1 should go to the Presidential Campaign Fund.

In Step 2 taxpayers mark their **filing status.**

- *Single* is for single persons with no dependents.
- *Married filing joint return* is for married persons who combine their income with their spouse's and file one return for two persons.
- *Married filing separate return* is for married persons who file individually.
- *Head of household* is for single persons with dependents.
- *Qualifying widow(er)* is for persons with dependents whose spouses have died recently. A qualifying widow(er) has the same tax rate as persons who are married and file jointly.

In Step 3 taxpayers must list their dependents and compute the number of exemptions. The number of exemptions (line 6e) should be figured carefully because a $2,000 deduction is allowed for each exemption (line 18).

In Step 4, taxpayers figure their total income. If a taxpayer has more than $400 of income from interest or dividends, a separate form must be completed and attached to Form 1040A.

In Step 5, taxpayers can deduct qualified contributions to an **Individual Retirement Account** (IRA) from their total income to find the **adjusted gross income.**

Follow these instructions to complete each step on the first page of Form 1040A. Use the form at the right.

COMPLETE STEP 1

1. Write the names Luiz J. and Eva M. Sanchez. Give them an address and social security numbers. They both want $1 to go to the Presidential Election Campaign Fund.

COMPLETE STEP 2

2. Check the box for Luis and Eva's filing status. They are filing a joint return.

COMPLETE STEP 3

3. Find the number of exemptions. Luis and Eva Sanchez have 3 dependent children, Carlos, Gloria, and Romeo. All of the children are older than age 5 and lived at home all year. Give the children social security numbers.

COMPLETE STEP 4

4. Luis's W-2 showed that he earned $18,530 in wages, while Eva earned $23,188. Write their total wages on Line 7.

5. Their joint savings account earned $263 interest. They also earned $130 interest on tax-free city savings bonds. Luis and Eva earned stock dividends of $301. Write these amounts on lines 8a, 8b, and 9.

6. Follow the instructions on line 11 to find the **total income** for Luis and Eva Sanchez.

COMPLETE STEP 5

7. Luis and Eva Sanchez can each deduct $2000 for IRA contributions. Complete each part of line 12 to find the **total adjustments.**

8. Complete line 13 to find the **adjusted gross income** for Luiz and Eva Sanchez.

> You may wish to make copies of this tax form to use for exercises on other pages. This form is a sample only. Because tax rules change frequently, new tax forms are distributed each year by the IRS.

Form **1040A**

Department of the Treasury—Internal Revenue Service

U.S. Individual Income Tax Return (X)   19—

OMB No. 1545-0085

Step 1
Label

Use IRS label. Otherwise, please print or type.

L A B E L   H E R E

Your first name and initial (if joint return, also give spouse's name and initial) — Last name

Your social security no.

Present home address (number, street, and apt. no.). (If you have a P.O. Box, see page 13 of the instructions.)

Spouse's social security no.

City, town or post office, state, and ZIP code

For Privacy Act and Paperwork Reduction Act Notice, see page 3.

Presidential Election Campaign Fund

Do you want $1 to go to this fund?. . . . . ☐ Yes   ☐ No

If joint return, does your spouse want $1 to go to this fund? ☐ Yes   ☐ No

Note: *Checking "Yes" will not change your tax or reduce your refund.*

Step 2
Check your filing status

(Check only one)

1 ☐ Single (See if you can use Form 1040EZ.)
2 ☐ Married filing joint return (even if only one had income)
3 ☐ Married filing separate return. Enter spouse's social security number above and spouse's full name here. _____
4 ☐ Head of household (with qualifying person). (See page 15.) If the qualifying person is your child but not your dependent, enter this child's name here._____
5 ☐ Qualifying widow(er) with dependent child (year spouse died ▶ 19____). (See page 16.)

Step 3
Figure your exemptions

(See page 16 of instructions.)

If more than 7 dependents, see page 19.

6a ☐ **Yourself**   If someone (such as your parent) can claim you as a dependent on his or her tax return, do not check box 6a. But be sure to check the box on line 15b on page 2.

6b ☐ **Spouse**

No. of boxes checked on 6a and 6b _____

c Dependents: 1. Name (first, initial, and last name)	2. Check if under age 5	3. If age 5 or older, dependent's social security number	4. Relationship	5. No. of months lived in your home in 1988

No. of your children on 6c who:
● lived with you _____
● didn't live with you due to divorce or separation (see page 19) _____

No. of other dependents listed on 6c _____

Attach Copy B of Form(s) W-2 here.

d If your child didn't live with you but is claimed as your dependent under a pre-1985 agreement, check here . . . . ▶ ☐

e Total number of exemptions claimed.

Add numbers entered on lines above ☐

Step 4
Figure your total income

Attach check or money order here.

7 Wages, salaries, tips, etc. This should be shown in Box 10 of your W-2 form(s). (Attach Form(s) W-2.) | **7** |

8a **Taxable** interest income (see page 22). (If over $400, also complete and attach Schedule 1, Part II.) | **8a** |

b **Tax-exempt** interest income (see page 23). (DO NOT include on line 8a.) | **8b** |

9 Dividends. (If over $400, also complete and attach Schedule 1, Part III.) | **9** |

10 Unemployment compensation (insurance) from Form(s) 1099-G. | **10** |

11 Add lines 7, 8a, 9, and 10. Enter the total. This is your **total income.** ▶ | **11** |

Step 5
Figure your adjusted gross income

12a Your IRA deduction from applicable worksheet. Rules for IRAs begin on page 24. | **12a** |

b Spouse's IRA deduction from applicable worksheet. Rules for IRAs begin on page 24. | **12b** |

c Add lines 12a and 12b. Enter the total. These are your **total adjustments.** | **12c** |

13 Subtract line 12c from line 11. Enter the result. This is your **adjusted gross income.** (If this line is less than $18,576 and a child lived with you, see "Earned Income Credit" (line 23b) on page 34 of instructions.) ▶ | **13** |

Form **1040A** (1988)

Form 1040A: Taxable Income and Credits

The second page of Form 1040A is shown on the page at the right.

In Step 6, taxpayers compute their taxable income. Line 16 is for the **standard deduction** which is based on a taxpayer's filing status. The amount for most persons is shown in this chart.

If your filing status is:	Your standard deduction is:
Single	$3,000
Married filing jointly or Qualifying widow(er)	$5,000
Married filing separately	$2,500
Head of household	$4,400

The standard deduction is greater for taxpayers who are older than 65 or blind. The deduction may be less for single persons who earn interest income and are claimed as dependents on another person's return.

On line 18 a taxpayer writes the **exemption amount,** $2000 times the number of exemptions on line 6e.

In Step 7, taxpayers compute their tax, credits, and payments. Line 21 allows a **credit for child and dependent care expenses** that enable the taxpayer to work. The credit is 20-30% of qualified expenses. The maximum credit is about $720 for one dependent, or $1440 for more than one dependent.

Line 23b allows an **earned income credit** for certain persons who earn less than $19,000 and have dependent children. The tax form includes a worksheet and tables for figuring the credit. The maximum credit is about $900. If a person qualifies for this credit, they can get a refund even if no taxes were withheld.

In Step 8, taxpayers compute the refund or amount owed.

In Step 9, taxpayers sign the form, write the date, and list their occupation.

Follow these instructions. Complete each step of the second page of Form 1040A for Luis and Eva Sanchez.

COMPLETE STEP 6
1. Copy the amount from line 13 and write it on line 14. Then use the chart at the left to find the **standard deduction** amount for Luis and Eva Sanchez. Write this amount on line 16. Then subtract and write the result on line 17.

2. Look back at the number of exemptions (line 6e). Multiply this number by $2000 and write the product on line 18. Subtract to find the taxable income on line 19.

COMPLETE STEP 7
3. Find the tax on the amount on line 19. Use the tax table on pages 148-149. Write the tax on line 20.

4. The Sanchez family can get a childcare credit of 20% of $4800, or $960. Write this amount on line 21. Subtract line 21 from 20 to find the total tax. Write this on line 22.

5. Luis and Eva Sanchez had two W-2 forms, and these amounts were withheld for federal tax: $1460.24, $1552.83. Write the total federal tax withheld, to the nearest dollar, on line 23a and on line 24.

COMPLETE STEP 8
6. Compare the amounts on line 22 and line 24, and find the difference. If line 24 is greater write the difference on line 25. This is the refund. If line 22 is greater write the difference on line 26. This is the amount owed.

COMPLETE STEP 9
7. The date is April 10, 1990. Luiz Sanchez is a security guard and Eva Sanchez is a teacher.

19— Form **1040A** Page 2

Step 6 **Figure your standard deduction,**	**14** Enter the amount from line 13.	14

15a Check if: { ☐ **You** were 65 or older ☐ Blind } **Enter number of**
{ ☐ **Spouse** was 65 or older ☐ Blind } **boxes checked ▶ 15a** ☐

b If someone (such as your parent) can claim you as a dependent, check here . . . . ▶15b ☐

c If you are married filing separately and your spouse files Form 1040 and itemizes deductions, see page 28 and check here . . . ▶15c ☐

	16 **Standard deduction.** See pages 28–29 for the amount to enter.	16
	17 Subtract line 16 from line 14. Enter the result. (If line 16 is more than line 14, enter -0-.)	17
exemption amount, and	**18** Multiply $1,950 by the total number of exemptions claimed on line 6e.	18
taxable income	**19** Subtract line 18 from line 17. Enter the result. (If line 18 is more than line 17, enter -0-.) This is your **taxable income.** ▶	19

Step 7

Figure your tax, credits, and payments (including advance EIC payments)

If You Want IRS To Figure Your Tax, See Page 29 of the Instructions.

Caution: If you are under age 14 and have more than $1,000 of investment income, check here . . . . ▶ ☐
Also see page 30 to see if you have to use Form 8615 to figure your tax.

20 Find the tax on the amount on line 19. Check if from:
☐ Tax Table (pages 37–42) or ☐ Form 8615 — 20

21 Credit for child and dependent care expenses. Complete and attach Schedule 1, Part I. — 21

22 Subtract line 21 from line 20. Enter the result. (If line 21 is more than line 20, enter -0-.) This is your **total tax.** ▶ 22

23a Total Federal income tax withheld—from Box 9 of your W-2 form(s). (If any is from Form(s) 1099, check here ▶ ☐ .) 23a

b Earned income credit, from the worksheet on page 35 of the instructions. Also see page 34. 23b

24 Add lines 23a and 23b. Enter the total. These are your **total payments.** ▶ 24

Step 8 **Figure your refund or amount you owe**	**25** If line 24 is more than line 22, subtract line 22 from line 24. Enter the result. This is the **amount of your refund.**	25
	26 If line 22 is more than line 24, subtract line 24 from line 22. Enter the result. This is the **amount you owe.** Attach check or money order for full amount payable to "Internal Revenue Service." Write your social security number, daytime phone number, and "1988 Form 1040A" on it.	26

Step 9

Sign your return

Under penalties of perjury, I declare that I have examined this return and accompanying schedules and statements, and to the best of my knowledge and belief, they are true, correct, and complete. Declaration of preparer (other than the taxpayer) is based on all information of which the preparer has any knowledge.

Your signature | Date | Your occupation

X

Spouse's signature (if joint return, both must sign) | Date | Spouse's occupation

X

Paid preparer's use only

Preparer's signature | Date | Preparer's social security no.

X

Firm's name (or yours if self-employed) | | Employer identification no.

Address and ZIP code | | Check if self-employed ☐

PAYING TAXES

Practice with Form 1040A

Complete each column of the chart. Line 25 or 26 in each column should be blank. Refer to a copy of Form 1040A.

	1.	2.	3.	4.	5.
NAME OF TAXPAYER	Bernard	H. Renner	P. Westin	Underwood	M. Chang
FILING STATUS	Married filing jointly	Single	Head of household	Married filing jointly	Married filing sep.
NUMBER OF EXEMPTIONS	4	1	3	2	1
Line 14 Adj. gross income	$40,185	$12,690	$23,603	$33,086	$15,952
Line 16 Standard deduction	5000	3000	4400	5000	2500
Line 17 Line 14 − line 16	*35,185*				
Line 18 Multiply $2000 by number of exemptions	*8000*				
Line 19 Taxable income	*27,185*				
Line 20 Tax from table. (See pages 143–149.)	*4076*				
Line 21 Credit for Childcare	1080	0	704	0	0
Line 22 Total Tax (Line 20 − line 21)	*2996*				
Line 24 Tax withheld plus earned income credit	2738	1385	1689	3287	1680
Line 25 Refund					
Line 26 Amount you owe					

6. Mr. and Mrs. Hannah had a total income of $40,634. They could deduct $4000 for IRA contributions. They claimed 4 exemptions and took the standard deduction of $5000. What was their taxable income?

Answer _____

7. Use the table on pages 148-149 to find Mr. and Mrs. Hannah's income tax. They can subtract a credit of 20% of $2370 for childcare. What is the tax liability of Mr. and Mrs. Hannah?

Answer _____

8. Tina Storment is filing as head of household. She qualifies for an earned income credit of $320. Her employer withheld $1,354 of federal tax. If the tax on her income is $1,504, does she owe or get a refund? How much?

Answer _____

9. Kasia Smith's W-2 showed earnings of $28,967. She also received $783 of interest income, but $125 of this was tax-exempt. What was Kasia's total taxable income?

Answer _____

PAYING TAXES
Real Estate Taxes

If you own a home or other property, you must pay **real estate** taxes to the city and/or county government. The money collected is used for schools and other local government services. The amount of real estate tax depends on the assessed value of the property and the tax rate for the location. The **assessed value** is found by multiplying the market value of the property by the rate of assessment (a percent). The market value is determined by the county assessor's office. The tax rate is determined by the city and/or county government.

The tax rate is often expressed in mills per dollar of assessed value. A **mill** is $\frac{1}{10}$ cent or $\frac{1}{1000}$ of a dollar. A yearly tax rate of 45 mills per dollar is equal to $45 per $1000 of assessed value.

EXAMPLE   The market value of a home is $75,400. The rate of assessment is 40% and the yearly tax rate is 52 mills. What is the assessed value of the property? How much real estate tax is owed for a year?

> Assessed value: 40% of $75,400 = $30,160
> Tax rate: 52 mills or $52 per $1000
> Assessed value in thousands: 30.16 (30,160 ÷ 1000)
> Real estate tax: $52 × 30.16 = $1568.32

If a home is mortgaged the lender may collect a portion of the real estate tax with each mortgage payment. The lender keeps the taxes in a special account called an **escrow** account, and pays each real estate tax bill when it is due. For the home described above, the lender would collect $\frac{1}{12}$ of $1568.32 each month. This is about $131 per month.

Complete the chart to find the yearly and monthly real estate tax for each home.

	Market Value	Rate of Assessment	Assessed Value	Assessed Value ÷ $1000	Tax Rate in Mills	Yearly Real Estate Tax	Monthly Real Estate Tax
1.	$58,000	30%	*$17,400*	*17.4*	46		
2.	$79,000	40%			55		
3.	$48,000	35%			38		
4.	$97,000	45%			27		
5.	$65,000	35%			16		
6.	$135,000	45%			40		
7.	$14,000	30%			51		
8.	$199,000	40%			48		

Itemized Deductions for Form 1040

Recall that most taxpayers can subtract a standard deduction from their income, based on their filing status. For example, from the table on page 155, the standard deduction for most single persons is $3000. Some persons, especially those with home mortgages, may pay less tax by **itemizing deductions** instead of using the standard deduction. A person who decides to itemize must use Form 1040 and complete Schedule A, *Itemized Deductions*.

Expenses that may be itemized include home mortgage interest, real estate taxes, state and local income taxes, moving expenses, and gifts to charity. If a person has very high medical expenses or casualty and theft losses, a portion of these expenses may be deductible. To decide whether to itemize deductions, add the deductible expenses. If the total is more than the standard deduction, it would be worthwhile to itemize.

EXAMPLE   Mr. and Mrs. Everett are filing a joint income tax return. The bank sent a statement showing that they paid $3672 in home mortgage interest and $1340 in real estate tax. Their W-2 forms showed that they paid $1410 in state and local income taxes. Also, they have receipts for gifts of $1300 to charity. Should they itemize deductions?

$$\$3672 + \$1340 + \$1410 + \$1300 = \$7722$$

Mr. and Mrs. Everett should itemize since $7722 is more than $5000, the standard deduction for a married couple filing jointly.

Find the total of each person's itemized deductions. Decide whether the person should itemize. Write *Yes* or *No*.

	Name	Standard Deduction	Itemized Deductions				Total	Should the person itemize?
			Mortgage Int.	Taxes	Charity	Other		
1.	A. Burns	$4400	$2378	$739	$745	0		
2.	W. West	$3000	$2702	$2450	$936	$320		
3.	R. Conley	$5000	0	$2877	$1293	$138		
4.	S. Evans	$3000	0	$600	$860	$207		
5.	F. Thomas	$5000	$4805	$3511	$4328	0		
6.	P. Moynan	$2500	$1790	$1584	$2310	$673		

7. In one year, Morris paid $2483 in medical expenses. His adjusted gross income was $21,380. He can deduct the portion of the medical expenses that exceeds 7.5% of $21,380. How much can he deduct for medical expenses? (Hint: Find $0.075 \times \$21,380$ and subtract the result from $2483.)   Answer _____

PAYING TAXES

Form 1040

Form 1040, called the long form, must be used by persons who itemize deductions on Schedule A. It must also be used by persons who have income from self-employment, farming, rental property, or certain other sources. Specialized tax forms or schedules must be completed and sent with Form 1040.

Persons who own a business or have self-employment income must complete Schedule C, *Profit or Loss from Business*, in addition to Form 1040. If the profit is over $400 they must also complete Schedule SE, *Social Security Self-Employment Tax*.

EXAMPLE Paula Albright is self-employed and made a profit of $28,648. Only $23,648 of her profit was taxable income. Her filing status is single. Use the table on pages 146–147 to find the amount of income tax she must pay. Then compute the self-employment tax, 13.3% of $28,648. What is Paula's total tax liability?

According to the table, she must pay $4295 tax on $23,648. The social security tax is 0.133 × $28,648 or $3810. Her total tax liability is $4295 + $3810, or $8105.

Solve.

1. Ricardo's business income from Schedule C was $8075. His income from interest and dividends was $723, and he had wages of $12,872. What was Ricardo's total income?

Answer _____

2. Ricardo must pay $2044 tax on his income. Also, he must pay 13.3% social security tax on his business income. (See Exercise 1.) What is his total tax liability?

Answer _____

3. Nancy's filing status is single. Her adjusted gross income for a year was $35,739. Find her taxable income by subtracting her itemized deductions, $5680, and one exemption, $2000.

Answer _____

4. Find Nancy's tax liability by using the table on pages 148–149. Nancy has no tax credits or other taxes. If $5,320 was withheld, does Nancy owe or get a refund? How much?

Answer _____

5. Chuck's filing status is head of household. His adjusted gross income for a year was $39,205. Find his taxable income by subtracting his itemized deductions, $5290, and 3 exemptions of $2000 each.

Answer _____

6. Chuck can take a tax credit of $770 for child-care expenses. Find the tax on Chuck's taxable income by using the table on pages 148–149. Then subtract the credit to find his tax liability. If $4408 was withheld, does Chuck owe or get a refund? How much?

Answer _____

PROBLEM-SOLVING STRATEGY

Select a Strategy

In this book, you have worked with several different problem-solving strategies. Some of them are listed in the box at the right.

PROBLEM-SOLVING STRATEGIES
Choose an Operation
Make a Table
Make a List
Use Estimation
Work Backwards
Find a Pattern
Make a Drawing
Use Guess-and-Check

Read the problem. Select a strategy from the box. Then solve.

1. In one year, Kingo Takata paid a total of $8400 for mortgage interest and real estate taxes. The mortgage interest was $3600 more than the taxes. How much mortgage interest did Kingo pay?

   Strategy _____

   Answer _____

2. Patty paid a total of $600 to an accountant who prepared tax forms for her business. Patty was charged $60 for the first hour plus $40 for each additional hour. How many hours did the job take?

   Strategy _____

   Answer _____

3. Manny Lincoln's W-2 form showed that his gross income for a year was $26,592. Suppose he earned the same amount each month. What was Manny's gross income per month?

   Strategy _____

   Answer _____

4. The checks in Vera's checkbook are numbered from 307 to 325. How many of the check numbers have digits with a sum less than 10? (Hint: The digits of 313 have a sum of $3 + 1 + 3 = 7$.)

   Strategy _____

   Answer _____

5. Mr. and Mrs. Zeller are filling out Schedule A, *Itemized Deductions*. They can deduct $3250 for taxes and $2500 for contributions to charity. They are also deducting mortgage interest. If their total deductions equal $10,950, how much mortgage interest are Mr. and Mrs. Zeller deducting?

   Strategy _____

   Answer _____

6. A large room in a tax preparation office is being separated into 8 foot square work areas. How many work areas can be made from a 16 ft by 24 ft space?

   Strategy _____

   Answer _____

Read the problem. Select a strategy from the box. Then solve.

7. A tax preparer charges $8 to fill out a 1040EZ and $15 to fill out a 1040A. In one evening, the tax preparer received $54 for completing some 1040EZ and 1040A forms. How many 1040EZ forms were completed?

Strategy _____

Answer _____

8. Raymond has four bills to pay, the phone, electric, rent, and a car payment. He is deciding the order in which to pay the bills. How many different orders are possible?

Strategy _____

Answer _____

9. Mabel must pay about 15% tax on her taxable income of $9812. About how much tax must she pay?

Strategy _____

Answer _____

10. Mr. and Mrs. Salefski spent a total of $4800 for childcare for their two girls. Childcare expenses for Jenny were twice as much as for Anna. How much was spent for childcare for Anna?

Strategy _____

Answer _____

11. Carola Delmar received three W-2 forms. The amounts withheld for federal tax were $1152, $294, and $487. What was the total federal income tax withheld?

Strategy _____

Answer _____

12. George Stefan made profits of $5824 from self-employment. He must pay 13.3% social security tax. About how much social security tax does he owe?

Strategy _____

Answer _____

13. There is a typing error in the section of the tax table shown below. Which amount is wrong? What might the correct amount be?

Taxable Income	Tax Amount (Single)
29,000-29,049	5,807
29,050-29,099	5,821
29,100-29,149	5,835
29,150-29,199	5,849
29,200-29,249	5,853

Strategy _____

Answer _____

14. There is a typing error in the section of the tax table shown below. Which amount is wrong? What might the correct amount be?

Taxable Income	Tax Amount (Head of Household)
7,400-7,449	1,114
7,450-7,499	1,112
7,500-7,549	1,129
7,550-5,599	1,136
7,600-7,649	1,144

Strategy _____

Answer _____

PAYING TAXES

Sales Tax

Most state governments and some local governments collect sales tax on purchases. The tax rate varies from state to state. The sales tax money is used to pay for the cost of government services.

EXAMPLE   Hubert buys a pizza for $8.69. If the sales tax rate is 6%, how much tax does he pay? What is the total cost?

6% of $8.69 = 0.06 × $8.69
           = $0.5214 or $0.53 (Note: Round up to the next cent.)

Total cost = $8.69 + $0.53 = $9.22

He pays 53¢ tax. The total cost is $9.22.

In some places, the rate of sales tax is lower on food and clothing. States also have different rules about what is taxable. For example, delivery fees and labor charges are taxed in some states but not others.

Find the sales tax and total cost for an item with the given price.

	Price	Sales Tax Rate	Sales Tax	Total Cost
1.	$200	4%		
2.	$12.98	6%		
3.	$88.45	5%		
4.	$9.73	7%		
5.	$37.82	4.5%		
6.	$284.35	6%		
7.	$10,850	5.5%		
8.	$0.86	6.5%		

9. Suppose you are buying three items with prices of $5.75, $15.34, and $42.99. The sales tax rate is 6%. How much sales tax will you pay?

10. A group of people went out to dinner. The bill was $76.35 plus 5.5% tax. They left a $12 tip. How much was paid in all? (Hint: Do not include sales tax on the tip.)

Answer _____

Answer _____

162

Excise Tax

Federal, state, and local governments may collect additional taxes, called **excise taxes,** on gasoline, cigarettes, liquor, and other specific items. These taxes may not be obvious to the consumer since some are paid by the manufacturer or supplier, but are passed on to the consumer as part of the purchase price.

Over 25% of the amount a customer pays for gasoline is excise tax. Gasoline taxes are collected by the federal government (9.1 cents per gallon), the states (from 7 cents to 17.4 cents per gallon), and local governments (amount varies). The money collected for gasoline taxes is used to build and repair streets and highways.

EXAMPLE   A station charges $1.45 per gallon for gasoline. Of that, 39¢ is excise tax. What percent of the price is excise tax?

39¢ is what percent of $1.45? Think of $1.45 as 145¢.

Divide 39 by 145. $39 \div 145 = 0.2689$

Write the decimal as a percent.   27%

Solve.

1. Suppose you buy 18 gallons of gasoline for $1.32 per gallon. What is your total cost? If the excise tax is 27 cents per gallon, how much excise tax is collected?

Answer _____

2. Suppose you buy 22 gallons of gasoline in a city that collects excise tax of 17¢ per gallon. If you pay $1.27 per gallon, what percent of the price is city excise tax?

Answer _____

3. Suppose you live in a state that collects 17.4¢ excise tax on a gallon of gasoline. If you buy 17.6 gallons of gasoline, how much state excise tax is collected?

Answer _____

4. Leroy buys 24.3 gallons of gasoline for $28.46. The price included $8.25 for excise tax. What percent of the price is excise tax?

Answer _____

5. Theresa lives in a state that collects 14.5¢ excise tax per gallon of gasoline. If she buys 19.3 gallons of gasoline, how much state excise tax is collected?

Answer _____

6. A customer paid $29.86 for 23.7 gallons of gasoline. The excise tax is 32.8¢ a gallon. How much would a gallon of gasoline cost without the excise tax?

Answer _____

Unit 7 Review

Solve.

1. Brent's monthly salary is $2,147. How much is withheld from Brent's pay each month for social security tax? Use a social security tax rate of 7.65%.

Answer _____

2. Walter's W-2 form showed that he earned $14,875 in wages. Of this, $297.50 was withheld for local tax. What percent of his wages were withheld for local tax?

Answer _____

3. Vernon is filing form 1040EZ. His adjusted gross income was $22,785. He takes a $3000 standard deduction and a $2000 personal exemption. What is his taxable income? If the tax rate is 15%, what is Vernon's tax liability?

Answer _____

4. Mr. and Mrs. Wheetley file a joint tax return using form 1040A. Their adjusted gross income is $45,308, and they take the $5000 standard deduction for married couples. If they claim 4 exemptions at $2000 each, what is their taxable income?

Answer _____

5. During the past year, $4381 of Ellen's pay was withheld for federal income tax. If her tax liability is $4628, will she owe or get a refund? How much?

Answer _____

6. The market value of a home is $48,000 and the rate of assessment is 45%. The tax rate is 52 mills ($52 per $1000). What is the yearly real estate tax?

Answer _____

7. Winona's filing status is head of household. She can deduct $4,359 in mortgage interest and real estate tax, $1,650 for charitable contributions, and $854 in state and local taxes. What is the total of these deductions? Should Winona itemize or take the standard deduction?

Answer _____

8. Nancy is self-employed and made a profit of $22,150 last year. She must pay $2572 in income tax. She also must pay social security tax of 13.3% of her profit. What is Nancy's total tax liability? Round to the nearest dollar.

Answer _____

9. Monroe bought three items of clothing costing $75.95, $28.65, and $15.88. The sales tax rate was 6.5%. How much sales tax did he pay on the three items? What was the total cost?

Answer _____

10. Kendra bought 16 gallons of gasoline for $1.34 per gallon. The price of each gallon included 29.3 cents for gasoline tax. What percent of the price was tax?

Answer _____

FINAL REVIEW

Find each answer.

	a	b	c	d	e
1.	3908 + 765	$65.74 + 3.86	2 +0.99	403 6795 +8579	0.03 3.33 +33.03
2.	42,833 − 1,976	$30.07 − 12.50	16 − 4.783	20,000 − 999	7064 − 195
3.	42 ×12	1.64 × 6	$7.49 × 15	8.8 ×0.9	$19.99 × 23
4.	24)1680	8)$56.32	4)3.21	1.2)66.48	0.75)2

Change each measurement.

	a	b	c
5.	45 m = _____ cm	651 kg = _____ g	3.8 L = _____ mL
6.	6 lb = _____ oz	52 in. = ___ ft ___ in.	15 pt = _____ c

Find each answer. Simplify.

	a	b	c	d
7.	$4 \times \frac{5}{12}$	$\frac{5}{6} \times \frac{1}{5}$	$4\frac{1}{2} \times \frac{2}{9}$	$\frac{1}{3} \times \frac{3}{16}$
8.	$\frac{1}{3} \div 15$	$\frac{7}{8} \div \frac{3}{4}$	$1\frac{1}{4} \div \frac{5}{16}$	$6\frac{1}{9} \div 1\frac{3}{8}$
9.	$\frac{2}{3} + \frac{3}{10}$	$1\frac{3}{4} + 4\frac{2}{5}$	$5 + 2\frac{3}{10}$	$3\frac{3}{16} + \frac{5}{8}$
10.	$\frac{5}{8} - \frac{1}{3}$	$6 - \frac{5}{9}$	$11 - 7\frac{1}{4}$	$6\frac{1}{9} - 2\frac{1}{8}$

Find each number.

<table>
<tr><td></td><td>a</td><td>b</td></tr>
<tr><td>**11.**</td><td>50% of 964</td><td>What percent of 1400 is 616?</td></tr>
<tr><td>**12.**</td><td>5% of what number is 45?</td><td>99% of 100</td></tr>
</table>

Solve.

13. Gary earns $210.40 for a 40-hour workweek. He earns $7.89 for each hour of overtime. How much does he earn for a 48-hour week?

Answer _____

14. Allissa is a computer technician who earns a monthly salary of $2750. What is her yearly salary?

Answer _____

15. Freddy sells office supplies. He earns a salary of $216 per work plus commission of 6% on all sales over $2000. One week he had sales of $6200. How much did he earn that week?

Answer _____

16. In one pay period, Jennifer had $624.80 in regular earnings. Her employer withheld $147.20 for taxes and $65.30 for insurance. What was Jennifer's take-home pay for that pay period?

Answer _____

17. Holly's disability insurance pays 60% of her salary for up to 52 weeks. If her weekly salary is $650 and she is disabled for 60 weeks, how much disability pay will she get?

Answer _____

18. A store owner bought lamps for $15.70 each and sold them for $27.95. The overhead was $10.80 per lamp. What was the profit on each lamp?

Answer _____

19. Pedro has a yearly income of $23,000. He budgets 12% for clothing. What amount does Pedro allow for his clothing budget?

Answer _____

20. Neil has a balance in his checking account of $639.47. If he writes a check for $249.44 and makes a deposit of $519.08, what will his new balance be?

Answer _____

21. Ingrid has $4500 in a 1-year CD at 6.4% interest. How much interest will she receive at the end of 1 year?

Answer _____

22. A farmer borrowed $4700 for 6 months at 12% interest. How much interest will the farmer pay on the loan?

Answer _____

Solve.

23. Rhonda borrowed $2300 to buy a stereo system. She will repay the loan in 24 installments of $109.37 each. How much interest will she pay on the loan?

Answer _____

24. Leland has an unpaid balance on his credit card of $450. If the finance rate is 1.8% per month, what is the finance charge on his balance?

Answer _____

25. Find the sticker price of a new car that has a base price of $9257, destination charge of $197, and these options:

Air conditioning $797
Luggage rack $149

Answer _____

26. Myron rented a compact car for $29 per day for 4 days and drove 540 miles. He was allowed 150 free miles per day, and was charged $0.20 for each additional mile. What was the total rental cost?

Answer _____

27. The yearly base premium for Heather's car insurance is $245.20. If her driver-rating factor is 2.4, how much is her yearly premium?

Answer _____

28. Suppose gasoline costs $1.45 per gallon. If your car gets 25 miles per gallon, find the cost of gasoline for a 700-mile trip.

Answer _____

29. A car was purchased for $10,900. Its value depreciated 45% in the first two years. Find the approximate trade-in value after two years.

Answer _____

30. Spencer can buy a monthly train pass for $76 or single-ride tickets for $2.50 each. He rides the train to and from work 20 days per month. How much money would he save each month by buying a monthly pass?

Answer _____

31. Greta buys a house for $70,000 and makes a down payment of $15,000. The mortgage payment is $11.01 per thousand of the loan amount. What is her monthly payment?

Answer _____

32. Last month Bridget's electric meter read 4205 kilowatt-hours. This month it reads 4840 kilowatt-hours. At 8¢ per kilowatt-hour, what will Bridget's electric bill be for the month?

Answer _____

Solve.

33. Bob wants to buy $70,000 worth of insurance for his new house. If the rate is $6.50 per $1000 of value, what will the insurance premium for his house be?

Answer _____

34. Estimate the cost of roofing a building if the roof area is 2100 square feet. The shingles will cost $68 per square and the labor charge is $75 per square. (One square of shingles covers 100 square feet.)

Answer _____

35. Torrey needed to hire a plumber to install a sink and a shower. The plumber charged for 3 hours and 15 minutes of labor. The rate was $45 for the first hour and $10 for each additional 15 minutes. How much did Torrey pay for the labor charge?

Answer _____

36. By paying cash instead of charging, Corwin bought a $650 desk for $611. What percent did he save?

Answer _____

37. Hannah's monthly salary is $1952. How much is withheld from Hannah's pay each month for social security tax? Use a social security tax rate of 7.65%.

Answer _____

38. Crystal is filing form 1040EZ. Her adjusted gross income was $20,508. She takes a $3000 standard deduction and a $2000 personal exemption. What is her taxable income? If the tax rate is 15%, what is Crystal's tax liability?

Answer _____

39. During the past year, $1964 of Chester's pay was withheld for federal income tax. If his tax liability is $2083, will he owe or get a refund? How much?

Answer _____

40. The market value of a home is $68,000 and the rate of assessment is 40%. The tax rate is 48 mills ($48 per $1000). What is the yearly real estate tax?

Answer _____

41. Xavier is self-employed and made a profit of $26,340 last year. He must pay $3651 in income tax. He also must pay social security tax of 13.3% of his profit. What is Xavier's total tax liability? Round to the nearest dollar.

Answer _____

42. Lana bought three items of clothing costing $15.35, $30.99, and $9.87. The sales tax rate was 5.5%. How much sales tax did she pay on the three items? What was the total cost?

Answer _____